Contents

* against a module denotes it as a module assessed only by terminal examination.

How to use this book

The revision guide contains the 12 modules that form the AQA Modular Science scheme. They cover the Foundation Tier of the syllabus.

You will need to learn and understand these six modules for module tests during the course:

AT2	AT3	AT4
Humans as organisms	*Metals*	*Energy*
Maintenance of life	*Earth materials*	*Electricity*

You will need to learn and understand these six modules for the terminal exam:

AT2	AT3	AT4
Environment	*Patterns of chemical change*	*Forces*
Inheritance and selection	*Structures and bonding*	*Waves and radiation*

You will also have to revise certain areas of the first group of six modules above for the terminal exam. These are very clearly marked by an orange tint, as shown here.

As you approach a module test or the terminal exam in your course, you can organise your work like this.

Work through the module or modules you need. Pace yourself – do one double page spread at a time and look back at the notes you have made in class on this topic.

Try the questions at the end of every double page spread to check that you really understand the topic.

Check your answers under *Answers to end of spread questions* (page 146). Go back over anything you find difficult.

Do the test style questions at the end of each module. These are in the same style as the questions you will have to do in the real end of module test or terminal exam, so they are very good practice.

Check your answers against the *Answers to module tests and terminal exam questions* (page 136). In terminal exam style questions take care to cover all the points needed to get full marks. Go back over areas you find difficult.

When you are revising for the terminal exams you will also need to revise the material marked with an orange tint in the other six modules. Revise these alongside modules in the same AT. For example, as you work through *Structures and bonding* or *Patterns of chemical change* in AT3 it would be a good idea to revise the terminal exam material in *Metals* or *Earth materials* at the same time.

The words in **red** are all key words you need to know. A useful revision idea would be to build up your own glossary of these as you work through the book. For quick reference to a word or topic use the *Index* (page 152) at the back of the book.

AQA

MODULAR

science

Nigel English

Heinemann

Heinemann Educational Publishers
Halley Court, Jordan Hill, Oxford, OX2 8EJ
a division of Reed Educational & Professional Publishing Ltd

Heinemann is a registered trademark of Reed Educational & Professional
Publishing Ltd.

OXFORD   MELBOURNE   AUCKLAND   JOHANNESBURG
BLANTYRE   GABORONE   IBADAN   PORTSMOUTH (NH)   CHICAGO

First published 1997

This edition published 2002

ISBN 0 435 100270

04 03 02
10 9 8 7 6 5 4 3 2 1

Edited by Sarah Ware and Allan Masson

Typeset and illustrated by Tech Set Ltd

Printed and bound in Italy by Printer Trento S.r.l

Acknowledgements
Cover photo by Digitalvision
Photos on pp 1, 43 and 87 by PhotoDisk

Life processes and living things

Humans as organisms

Maintenance of life

Environment

Inheritance and selection

Cells

What makes up animals and plants?
They are made up from cells. All animal cells have:

■ a **nucleus** – this controls everything a cell does

■ **cytoplasm** – this is the liquid where the cell's chemical reactions take place

■ a **cell membrane** that allows substances into and out of the cell.

We are not just made up of lots of disorganised cells. Cells are **specialised** to carry out different jobs (**functions**) within the body.

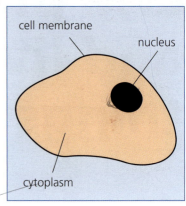

A typical animal cell

For example:

■ cells lining the windpipe have hair-like structures called cilia that move mucus up the windpipe

■ red blood cells are shaped like lozenges and have no nucleus, so more oxygen can get inside and be carried around the body

■ sperm cells have long tails so they can swim towards the egg cell

■ nerve cells are very long with many connections to other nerve cells so they can pass messages quickly through the body.

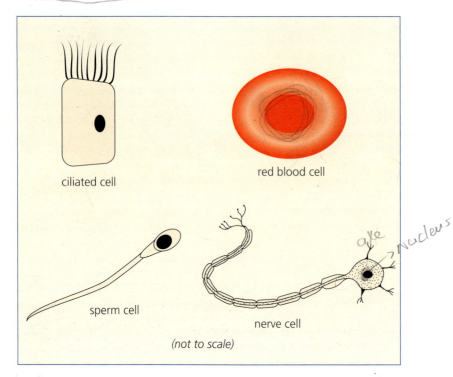

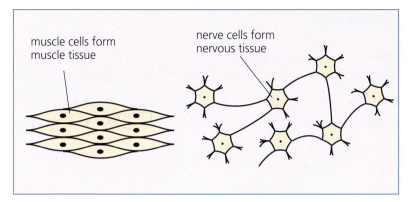

Types of tissue

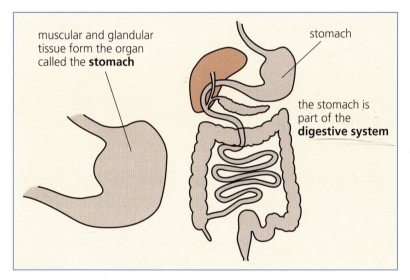

An organ is part of a system

Cells make up **tissues**, and different tissues make up **organs**. A group of organs forms a **system**. Specialised cells, tissues, organs and systems carry out different jobs in your body.

Questions

1 Copy and complete the table to show how different cells are adapted to help them carry out particular jobs.

Type of cell	What it does	How it is adapted
nerve	Passes information through the body	very long with many connections to other nerve cells
Sperm cell		has a long tail
Cilia cell	stops mucus building up on the lining of the windpipe	
red blood cell		

2 What are the **two** types of tissue that help form the stomach?

3 Muscle cells and sperm cells have different shapes to help them in the jobs they do. However, they have **three** structures in common. What are they?

Eating and digestion

Food has to get to the cells of the body so that they have the energy they need.

The food you eat contains insoluble lumps of starch (a carbohydrate), fats and proteins. These have to be broken down into small, soluble particles so your body can use them. This is called **digestion**. These small particles can then move into the blood, which transports them to the body cells.

This breakdown happens in the **digestive system**.

The digestive system

This has a number of organs including the gullet, stomach, liver, pancreas, small intestine and large intestine.

When you eat a meal, this is what happens.

■ Muscles in the wall of the gullet, stomach and intestines move the food along.

■ **Glands** produce **enzymes** that help to speed up the digestion (breakdown) of the food.

■ The salivary glands (in the mouth), pancreas and small intestine produce **amylase**. This speeds up the breakdown of starch into sugars.

■ The stomach, pancreas and small intestine produce **protease** enzymes. These speed up the breakdown of proteins into amino acids.

■ The pancreas and small intestine produce **lipase** enzymes. These speed up the breakdown of fats into fatty acids and glycerol.

The stomach also produces hydrochloric acid to kill most of the bacteria taken in with the food. The enzymes in the stomach work best in these acid conditions.

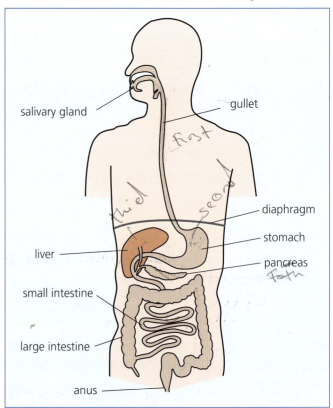

The human digestive system

Bile is produced in the liver and stored in the gall bladder. It is released from the liver into the small intestine. It does two things.

■ It makes the inside of the small intestine alkaline, which allows the enzymes there to work effectively. As food enters the small intestine it brings with it the acid added in the stomach. But enzymes in the small intestine can only work in alkaline conditions, so bile neutralises this acid and makes the juices in the small intestine alkaline.

■ It breaks down large fat globules into smaller ones, to make a larger surface area for enzymes to work on. This is known as **emulsification** and makes digestion faster.

Food is absorbed in the small intestine. This has many villi (*singular* villus), which look like fingers sticking out from inside the intestine wall. These increase the surface area for absorption of small, soluble food particles.

The body cannot digest some food, so this goes on into the large intestine. The large intestine absorbs most of the water from the food back into the body. The undigested food then passes out of the body through the anus as faeces.

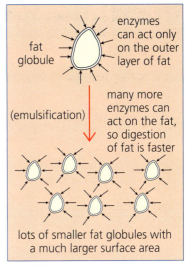

Emulsification

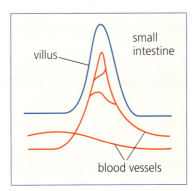

Villus

Questions

1 Copy out this table and fill in the gaps:

Name of organ	Enzymes it produces
salivary glands	
stomach	
pancreas	
small intestine	

2 A cheese sandwich has carbohydrate (in bread), fat (in butter) and protein (in cheese). This flow chart shows how the carbohydrate is broken down in the digestive system:

starch in bread → amylase in mouth and small intestine → glucose in blood

Draw similar flow charts for the digestion of the fat and protein from the sandwich.

3 What is the function of villi in the small intestine?

Breathing and respiration

Respiration

We breathe to take in oxygen from the air. Our body cells use the oxygen to release energy from food broken down in the digestive system. The food used is glucose, a type of sugar.

This is called **respiration**. Because it uses oxygen, it is called **aerobic** respiration.

Body cells produce carbon dioxide when they respire. We need to breathe out this gas. Carbon dioxide is a waste product of respiration. Water is also a waste product.

So respiration is:

glucose + oxygen $\longrightarrow$ **carbon dioxide + water + energy**

Sometimes, if there is a shortage of oxygen, body cells can respire **anaerobically** (that is, without oxygen) to produce the energy they need. The waste product from this is lactic acid, which quickly makes the muscles feel tired, so your body can't respire anaerobically for long!

The body now needs to break down this lactic acid. It needs extra oxygen to do this. This is known as the **oxygen debt**. It is why you pant or gasp after very hard exercise – your lungs are getting extra oxygen quickly.

Cover the page, then write down the **two** *things cells need for respiration and the* **three** *things they produce.*
Check your answer.

Why do we need energy?

We use the energy from food to:

- make our muscles contract so that we can move
- keep us warm when our surroundings are colder than we are – our body temperature needs to be kept the same all the time
- build up large, useful substances from the small, digested ones we take into our blood. We then use these substances to grow and to repair our bodies if they are damaged.

The breathing system

Oxygen passes into our blood through the lungs, and carbon dioxide passes out through the lungs.
The lungs are in the top part of your body (the **thorax**). They are separated from organs such as the stomach in the lower half of your body (the **abdomen**) by the **diaphragm**. The lungs are protected by a cage of bones called the **ribs**.

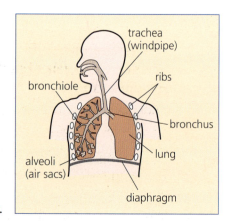

The breathing system

Air needs to get in and out of the lungs. To take air in the ribcage moves out and up and the diaphragm becomes flatter. To breathe out these changes are reversed.

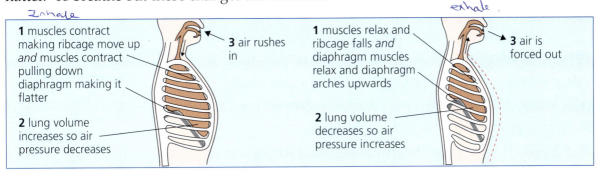

Inhale   *exhale .*

1 muscles contract making ribcage move up *and* muscles contract pulling down diaphragm making it flatter

3 air rushes in

2 lung volume increases so air pressure decreases

1 muscles relax and ribcage falls *and* diaphragm muscles relax and diaphragm arches upwards

3 air is forced out

2 lung volume decreases so air pressure increases

Breathing in   *… and breathing out*

Diffusion

The gases (oxygen or carbon dioxide) pass between the lungs and the blood through the millions of **alveoli** in the lungs. These are tiny air sacs with very thin walls. They are surrounded by lots of tiny blood vessels.

The gases **diffuse** through these thin walls. This means that the gases pass from the side where they are more concentrated to the side where they are less concentrated. When the oxygen in the blood reaches other cells in the body it enters the cells by **diffusion** through the cell membranes.

When you breathe in, the air in the alveoli has more oxygen than the blood – so oxygen diffuses into the blood. When it reaches the lungs, the blood has more carbon dioxide than the alveoli – so carbon dioxide diffuses into the alveoli.

All the alveoli together in the lungs provide a very large surface area for gas exchange.

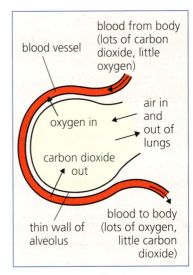

blood vessel

blood from body (lots of carbon dioxide, little oxygen)

air in and out of lungs

oxygen in

carbon dioxide out

thin wall of alveolus

blood to body (lots of oxygen, little carbon dioxide)

Gas exchange in alveoli

Questions

1 Copy and complete the sentences, choosing words from this list:

   water   oxygen   breathe   carbon dioxide   energy   glucose   respire

   Our cells use ~~oxygen~~ *energy* from the air to *respire* . This produces *oxygen*
   and the waste products are *carbon* and *dioxide* .

2 Our lungs are very delicate and important organs. Look at the diagram again. What protects the lungs from being crushed and damaged from outside?

3 Some types of exercise are called 'aerobic'. Suggest benefits to the body of aerobic exercise.

4 What movements do the ribs make that cause us to breathe in?

The circulatory system

This is really the body's transport system, with blood carrying substances around.

What is blood?

Blood consists of a liquid called **plasma** that carries red cells, white cells and platelets. Plasma also carries:

- carbon dioxide from the cells to the lungs
- digested food from the small intestine to the cells and organs of the body
- urea from the liver to the kidneys.

Red blood cells carry oxygen for respiration from the lungs to all the body organs.

White cells help defend the body against microorganisms (for example, bacteria) that may cause disease. They have a nucleus.

Platelets are bits of cells. They don't have a nucleus. When the skin is cut they help to form blood clots (these are the scabs that form over the cuts).

Cover the page then write down what white cells and platelets do. Check your answer.

The circulation system

We actually have two separate circulation systems – one to the lungs and one to the rest of the body.

The heart is a powerful muscle pumping blood around the body. It is divided into four parts or chambers. When blood enters the heart it goes into an **atrium**. The atrium contracts and squeezes the blood through into a **ventricle**. The ventricle contracts and forces the blood out of the heart.

Valves in the heart make the blood flow in the right direction. They stop the blood flowing backwards.

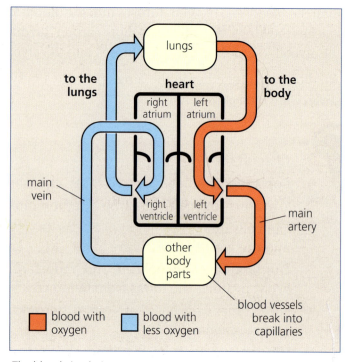

The blood circulation system

The blood vessels

Arteries are large vessels that carry blood away from the heart. The heart pumps out blood with great force and arteries have thick, muscular, elastic walls to cope with this high pressure.

Veins are also large vessels that bring blood back to the heart. The pressure from the heartbeat is low by the time the blood gets to the veins, so they have thinner walls than arteries. They also have valves along their length to prevent the backflow of blood, especially when it is coming back from your feet!

Capillaries are very narrow, thin-walled blood vessels that run through the organs of the body. Blood flows into them from the arteries and out to the veins.

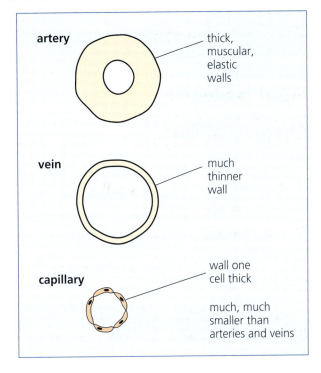

The thin walls allow substances to get in and out of the capillaries. For example, oxygen and glucose go from the capillaries to the body cells, and carbon dioxide and water come from the body cells to the blood.

This happens by diffusion (like the movement of gases through the alveoli in the lungs). When water, sugar and other nutrients are more concentrated in the blood than in the cells, they pass through the cell membrane into the cell. The greater the difference in concentration, the faster diffusion happens.

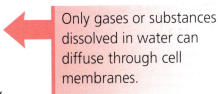

Only gases or substances dissolved in water can diffuse through cell membranes.

Questions

1 Copy this table and fill in the gaps.

Parts of the blood	What they do	Structure
plasma		liquid
red cells		no nucleus, contains haemoglobin
white cells		
	help heal cuts	

2 Why do arteries need thick muscular walls?

Disease

What causes disease? One of the main causes is when **microorganisms** such as certain bacteria and viruses get into the body. These cause a whole range of illnesses, from the common cold to meningitis and AIDS.

Microorganisms

Bacterial cells have cytoplasm surrounded by a cell membrane. All of this is surrounded by a cell wall. They have no nucleus. Usually, the genes that allow a cell to reproduce and make copies of itself are in its nucleus. In bacteria, the genes are in the cytoplasm.

Viruses are much smaller than bacteria. They are very different from cells. They have a protein coat surrounding a few genes. They can reproduce only inside the living cells of organisms.

If large numbers of microorganisms (bacteria or viruses) enter your body then you may catch a disease. The microorganisms can reproduce very quickly inside your body so that there are soon millions of them. They may produce poisons (also called **toxins**) that make you feel ill.

If a virus reproduces in one of your cells, the cell will be damaged.

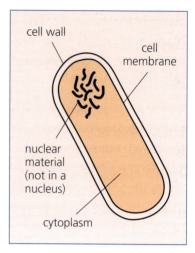

A bacterium

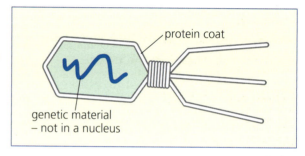

A virus

Defence against disease

The best way is to stop the bugs (microorganisms) getting in! Your body can do this in several ways.

- Skin acts as protection – if you have a cut, microorganisms can get straight through into your blood.

- Blood clots and forms scabs, which seal cuts in the skin and stop microorganisms getting in.

- Air passages in your nose and lungs have thick, sticky mucus on their surfaces inside to trap microorganisms – when you blow your nose or cough you are getting rid of these trapped microorganisms.

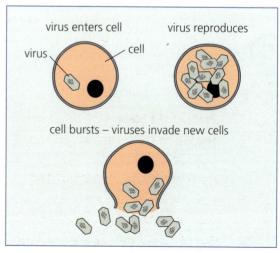

A virus reproducing

But if the microorganisms manage to get in then white cells spring into action. They:

- ingest (eat) the bacteria
- produce **antibodies** that help destroy particular bacteria or viruses
- produce **antitoxins** to neutralise (get rid of) the poisons (toxins).

If your body is infected with a particular microorganism, the white cells produce particular antibodies to fight it. The next time that a microorganism invades your body, the white cells can produce the right antibodies much more quickly – your body is now **immune** to the infection.

Immunity can be given to your body by **vaccination**. This is when you are injected with a less harmful or dead form of a particular microorganism (for example measles). It makes the white cells produce the necessary antibodies, and prepares your body to fight the microorganism if it gets into your body in the future.

Disease and lifestyle

How do you come into contact with harmful microorganisms?

Here are two ways.

- When ill people cough or sneeze they release a fine spray that contains microorganisms. If you breathe these in you risk catching the same illness.
- If you eat food prepared in unhygienic conditions or drink unclean water, you may become ill. Unclean water is often found when large numbers of people are crowded into one place without any sewage treatment systems. It can carry the killer disease cholera, which spreads very fast.

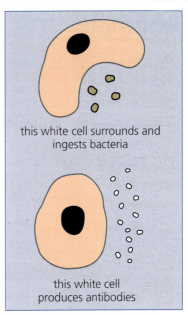

this white cell surrounds and ingests bacteria

this white cell produces antibodies

White blood cells attack invading microorganisms

People have known about infectious diseases for centuries, but it was only in the 1800s that they began to find out what caused them and how they spread.

Cholera was a new disease to hit Britain in the 1830s. Most doctors thought it was spread by touch or 'bad air'. A turning point came in 1854, when hundreds of Londoners died in a cholera epidemic. Dr John Snow thought the disease might be passed through water, so he recorded where each of the victims lived. By plotting this information on a local map he saw that they all got their water from a pump in Broad Street. He persuaded the authorities to have the pump handle removed, and quickly the epidemic began to subside.

Questions

1 Draw a spider diagram to show all the defences the human body has against microorganisms. Put **the body** at the centre of the diagram.

2 A bacterial cell has **two** things that are different from an ordinary animal cell. What are they?

3 'Coughs and sneezes spread diseases.' How?

Module test questions

1 These sentences are about the blood system.

Choose words from the list for each of the spaces 1–4 in the sentences.

white cells
platelets
plasma
red cells

Oxygen is carried by *red cells* ____**1**____ in the blood. The liquid part of the blood is called ____*Plasma*___**2**___. Normally the skin keeps microorganisms out, but if the skin is cut ___*platelets*___**3**___ help to form blood clots. If microorganisms do get into the blood then ____**4**____ help defend the body. *White cells.*

2 The diagram shows part of the breathing system.

Choose words from the list for each of the labels 1–4 on the diagram.

2 **bronchus**
1 **trachea**
4 **rib**
3 **air sac**

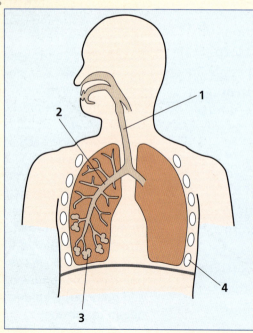

3 This is a diagram of the gut.

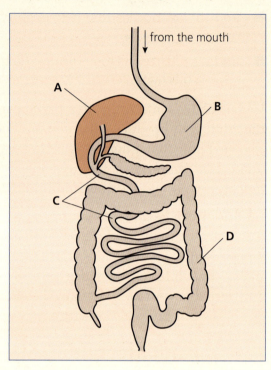

from the mouth

1. In which part is bile produced?
   A **B** **C** **D**

2. In which part does most absorption of water take place?
   A **B** **C** **D**

3. In which part are the products of digestion mainly absorbed?
   A **B** **C** **D**

4. In which part does fat digestion take place?
   A **B** **C** **D**

4 Which **two** of the following statements are true about the stomach?

   A it produces lipase enzymes
   B digested food is absorbed through its walls
   C the conditions inside it are acid
   D it produces carbohydrase and protease enzymes
   E it produces protease enzymes.

5 Which **two** of the following statements are true about the circulation system?

   A it transports carbon dioxide from the organs to the lungs

   B it transports oxygen from the organs to the lungs

   C it transports urea from the kidneys to the liver

   D it transports digested food from the small intestine to the organs

   E it transports digested food from the organs to the small intestine.

6 This is a diagram of the circulatory system.

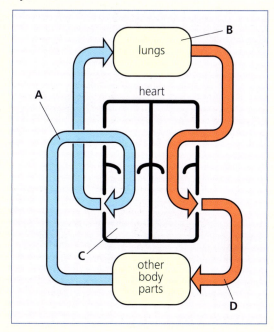

1. In which part of the system is oxygen picked up?

   A B C D

2. Which part of the system pumps deoxygenated blood?

   A B C D

3. Which part of the system carries oxygenated blood to the body?

   A B C D

4. Which part of the system is carrying blood at low pressure back to the heart?

   A B C D

7 This question is about respiration.

1. What are the **two** waste products of respiration?

   A oxygen and water

   B carbon dioxide and water

   C oxygen and carbon dioxide

   D carbon dioxide and nitrogen.

2. Which best describes respiration?

   A the release of energy from food

   B the release of energy from oxygen

   C the exchange of gases

   D the breathing in of oxygen and out of carbon dioxide.

3. The proper name for an air sac in the lungs is:

   A bronchus

   B bronchiole

   C larynx

   D alveolus.

4. Which of the following is not an adaptation of the lungs that helps gas exchange?

   A good blood supply

   B dry surfaces

   C large surface area

   D thin walls.

How do plants make their food?

Plant and animal cells

Plant and animal cells are made up from different parts. They have some parts in common:

- a **nucleus** – controlling what the cell does
- **cytoplasm** – liquid where cell reactions take place
- **cell membrane** – allowing substances in and out of the cell (for example, oxygen).

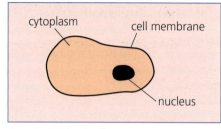

A typical animal cell

Plant cells have three parts that animal cells never have:

- **cell wall** – so that the cell stays the same rigid shape
- **chloroplasts** – that absorb energy from light to make food for the plant
- a **vacuole** – that contains a liquid called the cell sap.

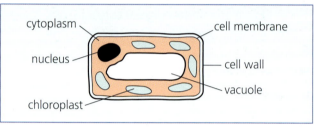

A typical plant cell

Not all of the millions of cells in a plant are the same. Like animals, plants have specialised cells to do certain jobs. A group of specialised cells is called a **tissue**. Different tissues group together to form an **organ**. A leaf is an example of a plant organ.

*Cover the page, then write down which **three** parts all cells have and what they do.*
Check your answer.

xylem vessels are tubes formed from chains of dead cells – they carry water and minerals up the plant.

pairs of guard cells on the lower surface (of most leaves) – they allow the exchange of gases.

stoma

guard cells

soil particles

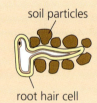

root hair cell

these cells are able to take in water from the soil – they provide a large surface area.

Making food

Unlike animals plants make their own food. They do so by **photosynthesis**. This produces sugar (glucose) for the plant to use. It is done like this:

- green **chlorophyll** in the chloroplasts traps (absorbs) light, which provides energy
- this energy is used to make carbon dioxide and water into sugar (glucose)
- oxygen is given off as a waste product.

carbon dioxide + water $\xrightarrow{\text{light energy}}$ **glucose + oxygen**

Plants usually store the glucose as starch. This is insoluble (it does not dissolve in water).When the plants need the starch for energy (or growth) they change it back into glucose.

What do plants need for photosynthesis?
Plants need:

- carbon dioxide
- water
- some warmth
- light
- nitrate (for healthy growth).

The rate or speed of photosynthesis can be slowed down (limited) by:

- low temperature
- shortage of carbon dioxide
- too little light.

Temperature, carbon dioxide and light are the **limiting factors** of photosynthesis.

Imagine you own a greenhouse. You might decide to heat it to make your plants grow faster. But this would only work if there was enough carbon dioxide and light getting into the greenhouse. If either light or carbon dioxide was in short supply the plants couldn't photosynthesise any faster, no matter how much you heat the greenhouse. You would be wasting your money!

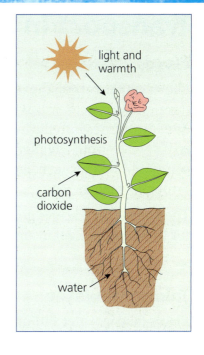

Respiration
Plant cells respire just like animal cells.
They use some of the glucose made during photosynthesis to release energy.

Questions

1 You have lots of cells in your body. There are **three** structures plant cells have that none of your cells have. What are they and what do they do?

2 This question is about photosynthesis. Copy and complete the sentences, choosing words from this list:

   carbon dioxide   oxygen   chlorophyll   water   glucose

   Plants take in _oxygen_ and _water / carbon dioxide_ in order to photosynthesise. The _chlorophyll_ in the leaves traps the Sun's energy. They produce _glucose_, which they store as starch. The waste gas they produce is called _carbon dioxide_.

3 Why don't people have to cut their lawns in the winter?

Transport in plants

Gases

Plants get the carbon dioxide they need for photosynthesis through holes in their leaves, called **stomata**. The carbon dioxide diffuses into the leaves and then into the cells (that is, it spreads from a higher concentration to a lower concentration). Oxygen also moves in and out of the leaves through stomata.

The flat shape of leaves gives them a bigger surface area for these gases to get in and out.

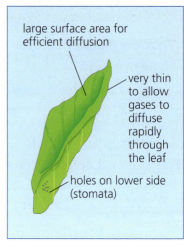

large surface area for efficient diffusion

very thin to allow gases to diffuse rapidly through the leaf

holes on lower side (stomata)

Cross-section through a leaf

Taking in water

Plants take in water through their roots. Most of this is absorbed by the **root hair cells**.

Plants also take in mineral salts with the water. These include nitrates, which are needed for healthy growth. Flowering plants transport water and minerals to their stems and leaves through xylem tissue.

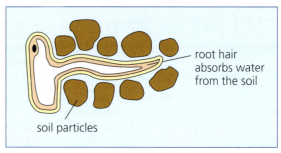

root hair absorbs water from the soil

soil particles

A root hair cell

Osmosis

Water moves into the root hair by **osmosis**. Look at the diagram. There is a greater concentration on the right of the membrane (the part that is only water). There is a lower concentration on the left (the part that is sugar and water). You know that molecules move from a greater concentration to a lower concentration (diffusion). Osmosis is simply the diffusion of water molecules.

In the diagram, you can see that water molecules can pass both ways through the membrane but the sugar molecules can't pass through at all. The membrane is **partially permeable**. However, more water molecules will move to the left, into the sugar solution, than the other way. We call this a **nett movement** of water molecules.

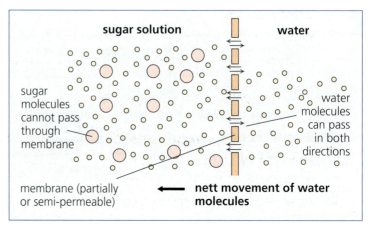

sugar solution water

sugar molecules cannot pass through membrane

water molecules can pass in both directions

membrane (partially or semi-permeable)

nett movement of water molecules

Losing water

Plants lose water from their leaves because it evaporates through the stomata. This is called **transpiration**. Transpiration happens fastest on hot, dry and windy days.

If plants lose water faster than their roots can replace it, they **wilt**. This is especially dangerous for young plants, which are mostly held up by water in their cells.

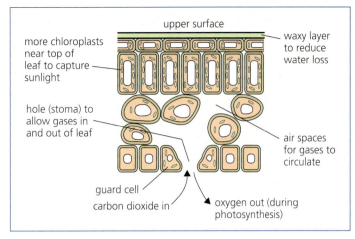

Inside a leaf

So plants have ways of cutting down the amount of transpiration (water loss):

- most plants have a thick, waxy layer on their leaves to stop them losing too much water (for example, plants that live in very hot, dry conditions have thicker waxy layers)
- the stomata are surrounded by **guard cells** that control their size. These close if too much water is lost.

Food

The sugars made in the leaves by photosynthesis are transported to the rest of the plant by **phloem** tissue, especially to growing parts or places where the sugar is stored as starch.

Cover the page, then write down what phloem transports. Check your answer.

Questions

1. Copy and complete the sentences, choosing words from this list:

   xylem   sugars   phloem   nutrients   water

   In a plant it is the _____ that transports _____ and _____ from the roots to all parts. Photosynthesis results in the production of _____ , which are transported by _____ to all parts of the plant, but particularly to areas where there is a lot of growth.

2. How can a leaf reduce the amount of water it transpires (that is, water that evaporates from its surface)?

3. How would you describe osmosis?

How do plants respond?

Plants react to their surroundings (respond) in many ways. They can respond to light, moisture and to gravity:

- **shoots** grow towards the light and away from the force of gravity
- **roots** grow towards moisture and the force of gravity.

Plant hormones make these things happen. Hormones are chemical messengers. Animals have hormones as well – but they are different to plant hormones.

Hormones collect on the lower sides of shoots and roots. In shoots, this makes the lower side grow faster, so the shoot bends up as it grows. In roots the hormones slow down the growth on the lower side, so the root grows down.

Other plant hormones control growth and reproduction. We use them to:

- help plant cuttings to grow roots and produce large numbers of plants quickly
- ripen fruit at the time the grower wants it to ripen
- kill weeds in the garden by causing them to grow so rapidly that they die.

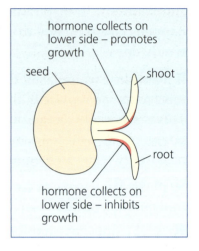

hormone collects on lower side – promotes growth

seed

shoot

root

hormone collects on lower side – inhibits growth

*Cover the page and write down **three** ways gardeners and growers use plant hormones. Check your answer.*

How do humans respond?

Reacting to our surroundings

We must react in the right way. If you touch a hot pan it is no good scratching your leg! You always make a **coordinated** response.

Changes to our surroundings are called **stimuli** (for example, looking at a bright light, touching a sharp object). These changes are detected by **receptors** (for example, the eyes detect the bright light, nerve endings in the skin detect pain).

We can respond to many different stimuli.

Receptors in	are sensitive to	which means
eye	light	you can see
ear	sound	you can hear
ear	changes in position	you can balance
tongue and nose	chemicals	you can taste and smell
skin	pressure and temperature	you can feel heat and different textures

All these receptors send information to your brain. It is your brain that coordinates your response (makes sure that you do the right thing).

Some responses to stimuli happen very quickly and automatically. These are called **reflex actions**. A simple reflex action happens like this:

- a receptor is stimulated
- it sends messages to the spinal cord (or brain) through a **sensory neurone** (a special type of nerve cell)
- the spinal cord (or brain) sends messages to a muscle or a gland through a **motor neurone**
- the muscle responds by contracting, or the gland makes a hormone or enzyme.

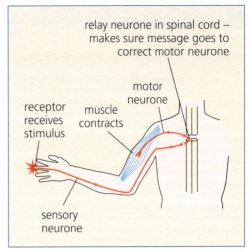

A reflex arc

The eye

This is how you see:

- light enters the eye through the cornea
- the cornea *and* lens focus light on the retina
- the receptor cells of the retina send messages along the optic nerve to the brain.

The optic nerve is a bundle of **sensory neurones** (nerves). They carry messages in the form of **impulses**.

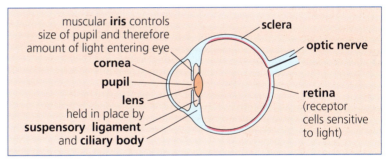

The structure of the eye

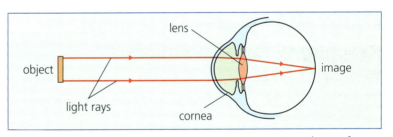

How the eye focuses

Questions

1 The sentences below are about growth in plants. Copy and complete the sentences, choosing words from this list:

   downwards   lower   quickly   hormones   upwards   upper   slowly

   If a shoot starts growing horizontally from a seed the growth _____ collect on the _____ side. This causes the shoot on that side to grow more _____ and therefore the shoot grows _____ .

2 What is the job of each of these parts of the eye?

   a iris   **b** retina   **c** optic nerve   **d** lens.

3 What is a sensory neurone?

Reacting to things inside us

We also react to things happening inside us. This is known as controlling our internal environment.

The body produces substances that it has to get rid of, or **excrete**. These include:

- carbon dioxide – a waste product of respiration, excreted through the lungs when we breathe out.

- urea – produced by the liver (from amino acids we don't want) and excreted by the kidneys in the urine, which is stored in the bladder until we can get rid of it.

Hormones

A lot of what happens inside us is controlled by **hormones**. These are chemicals produced by glands and carried by the blood. There are many different hormones with different jobs. Each hormone acts on one particular organ.

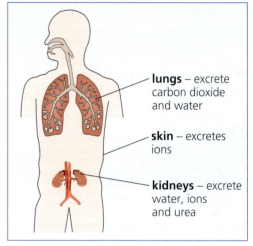

Excretion from the body

lungs – excrete carbon dioxide and water

skin – excretes ions

kidneys – excrete water, ions and urea

Keeping a balance

Some things inside us need to be kept at a constant level. These include water content, ions and temperature.

Water content

We lose water through our lungs when we breathe out and through our skin when we sweat. If we lose too much and the amount of water in our bodies drops too low, we have to take in more by eating and drinking. If we have too much water, our kidneys remove the extra (excess) and it leaves the body in the urine.

Ions

We lose mineral ions (for example, iron, calcium and sodium) through sweat when we are hot. If we have too many ions our kidneys remove the excess and they leave the body in the urine.

Temperature

Our bodies must stay the same temperature inside because our enzymes work best at this temperature. If we get too hot or too cold they won't work and we will die. Sweating helps to keep the body cool. On hot days we sweat more so we need to drink more.

Sugar

Sugar is essential to our bodies. It supplies all our body cells with the energy they need. But we must keep the amount of sugar in our blood at the right level. If we have too much or too little it can be fatal.

So how do we keep the amount of sugar at the right level? Two hormones, **insulin** and **glucagon**, control the level. They are both produced by the pancreas. Insulin stops the sugar level rising too high, and glucagon stops it from falling too low.

Sometimes the pancreas does not produce enough insulin and this causes the disease **diabetes**. People with diabetes have to control the sugar in their diet carefully and may inject insulin into their blood to control the problem.

When the sugar level in your blood rises too high your pancreas releases insulin.
When the sugar level falls too low your pancreas releases glucagon.

Drugs

There are many different drugs. Some drugs are illegal. You need to know about three types.

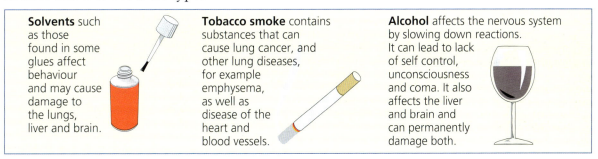

Solvents such as those found in some glues affect behaviour and may cause damage to the lungs, liver and brain.

Tobacco smoke contains substances that can cause lung cancer, and other lung diseases, for example emphysema, as well as disease of the heart and blood vessels.

Alcohol affects the nervous system by slowing down reactions. It can lead to lack of self control, unconsciousness and coma. It also affects the liver and brain and can permanently damage both.

Drugs affect the body in a way that some people can become **addicted** to them. This means they can't cope without the drug, and suffer **withdrawal symptoms** that make them feel worse when they don't take the drug. For example, many smokers are addicted to nicotine in tobacco.

Tobacco smoke also contains carbon monoxide. This affects how much oxygen your blood can carry. For pregnant women, this can mean the baby not getting enough oxygen and so being born underweight.

Questions

1 Make a table showing **three** substances that are excreted by the body, and where in the body they are excreted.

2 What happens to the level of sugar in the blood if, during a meal, you eat a lot of food containing sugar.

3 Which **two** organs do both solvents and alcohol affect?

4 A large number of people die every year from lung cancer. Which other system in the body does smoking badly affect?

5 How does alcohol affect the nervous system?

Module test questions

1 The table is about cells and the jobs the different parts have.

Match words from the list with each of the numbers 1–4 in the table.

nucleus
cytoplasm
cell wall
chloroplast

	Job
1	traps the Sun's energy for photosynthesis
2	controls the activities of a cell
3	maintains the cell's rigid shape
4	where the cell reactions take place

2 These sentences are about transport systems in a plant.

Choose words from the list for each of the spaces 1–4 in the sentences.

xylem
stomata
guard cells
phloem

Carbon dioxide is able to enter a plant through holes in the leaves called ____1____ . The size of these holes is controlled by the ____2____ . Water taken in by the roots is transported by the ____3____ to the rest of the plant. At the same time ____4____ is carrying sugars from the leaves to other parts of the plant.

3 This questions is about how humans respond.

Match words from the list with each of the numbers 1–4 in the table.

tongue   ear   skin   nose

	Job
1	has receptors sensitive to smell
2	has receptors sensitive to sound
3	has receptors sensitive to taste
4	has receptors sensitive to pressure and temperature

4 The diagrams are of a plant cell and an animal cell.

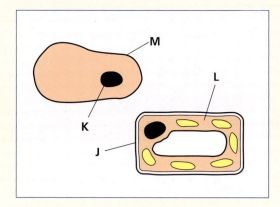

Match words from the list with each of numbers 1–4 in the table.

4 **cell membrane**
1 **cell wall**
3 **cytoplasm**
2 **nucleus**

	Part of cell
1	structure J
2	structure K
3	structure L
4	structure M

5 Which **two** of these substances are the products of photosynthesis?

   A starch
   B glucose
   C water
   D oxygen
   E carbon dioxide.

6 Which **two** of these substances control blood sugar?

    A urea
    B glucagon
    C starch
    D glucose
    E insulin.

7 This is a diagram of the eye.

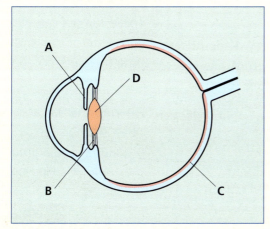

1. Which part is muscular and controls the amount of light entering the eye?

    A B C D

2. Which part contains light sensitive cells?

    A B C D

3. Which part of the eye focuses light?

    A B C D

4. Which part holds the lens in place?

    A B C D

8 This question is about plant hormones.

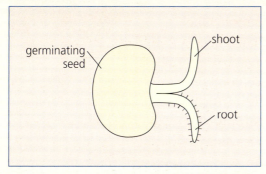

1. Shoots bend upwards as they grow because:

    A growth hormone collects on the lower side – this increases the speed of growth, so the lower side grows more slowly

    B growth hormone collects on the lower side – this increases the speed of growth, so the lower side grows more quickly

    C growth hormone collects on the upper side – this increases the speed of growth, so the upper side grows more quickly

    D growth hormone collects on the upper side – this increases the speed of growth, so the upper side grows more slowly.

2. Roots grow downwards because:

    A the same amount of hormone increases growth rate in roots

    B hormone collects on both upper and lower sides equally

    C the hormone collects on the lower side slowing growth

    D the hormone collects on the upper side increasing growth.

3. Which of the following is not a use of plant growth hormones?

    A helping to produce flowers all of the same colour

    B helping cuttings to root

    C help to ripen fruit when the grower wants

    D as weedkillers.

4. To which force do plant roots respond?

    A light

    B water

    C nutrients

    D gravity.

Choosing a home

Animals and plants are **adapted** to help them survive in the places they normally live.

For example, animals in very cold, arctic areas need to keep warm. They tend to have:

- a large body size compared to their surface area (to reduce heat loss)
- a thick insulating coat
- a large amount of body fat.

These features would make life in the desert very difficult! Animals that live in hot, dry climates have different adaptations. For example, camels store fat in their humps. Many animals wherever they live use **camouflage**, either so that predators find it more difficult to see them, or prey don't spot them coming!

Plants living in hot and dry desert areas have adaptations to prevent too much water loss. These might include:

- waxy surfaces to their leaves to reduce evaporation
- needles instead of leaves (for example, a cactus) to reduce the surface area from which water can be lost
- stomata that are sheltered from the wind to prevent too much transpiration.

The physical factors that may affect organisms include:

- temperature
- light
- water
- oxygen
- carbon dioxide.

These factors can vary with time of day and time of year.

Animals that kill and eat other animals are predators. The animals they eat are called prey.

Competition

Plants often compete with each other for space, water and nutrients. For example, a new seedling trying to grow underneath an oak tree is likely to die. The tree's leaves shade it from a lot of the sunlight, and the tree's roots take most of the water and nutrients from the soil. Plants need space to get the water, nutrients and light they need. Animals often compete with each other for space, food and water. For example, birds have their territories, which they protect. They are actually protecting their supply of food and water and, at breeding times, their mates and offspring.

oak tree

this seedling may die if there is not enough light, moisture or nutrients

How big can a population get?

The size of a population of organisms depends on the following things (factors):

■ how much food or nutrients are available

■ how much competition there is for the food or nutrients

■ competition for light (especially for plants)

■ how many of the animals are eaten, or how many plants are eaten (grazed) by animals

■ how much disease there is.

However, other things affect the size of populations in a group (community) of organisms:

■ If the number of prey increases (for example, mice), more food is available for its predators (for example, owls). So the numbers of predators (owls) may increase.

■ If the number of predators increases, more food is needed. So the numbers of prey will go down – more mice will be eaten by the owls!

This usually means that populations of different organisms (for example, in a hedgerow) are kept in balance. They remain stable.

Population – the total number of that type of organism in an area. For example, the number of badgers in a wood.

Community – all of the organisms living in a particular area. For example, all of the organisms, including plants, living in a pond.

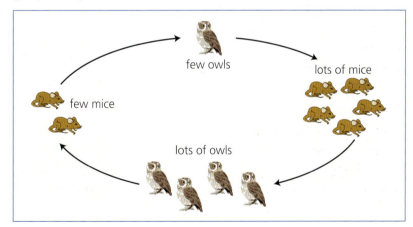

A population cycle

Questions

1 There is a population of owls in your area. The owls eat small animals and birds. Which of these factors are likely to result in an increase in the owl population?

   more light   **fewer small animals**
   more disease   **more plant growth**
   more small birds   **less water**

2 If the owl population rises, what is likely to happen to the number of small animals?

3 How is a shark adapted to catch prey?

4 An oak tree produces many acorns, which fall to the ground. Why do so few grow into oak trees?

Food chains, webs and pyramids

Radiation (heat and light) from the Sun provides the energy for photosynthesis. Plants can capture this energy and use it to make food. They store it in the substances that make up plant cells. This is why plants are called **producers**.

Animals either eat plants or each other. They are known as known as **consumers**.

A food chain

Food chains

A **food chain** is a way of showing what eats what.

Food chains always start with plants producing food for all other organisms.

Food webs

In any community, it is very rare to have a simple food chain. For example, many animals eat grass and lots of animals eat rabbits. It's not much of a life being a rabbit!

If we connect up all the food chains we can make a **food web**.

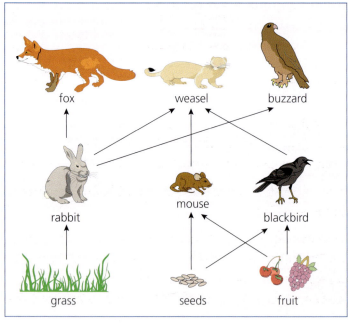

A food web

Pyramids of numbers

Food chains and webs show us how energy and material are transferred from one organism to another. The numbers of organisms involved at each stage of a food web can be shown as a **pyramid of numbers**.

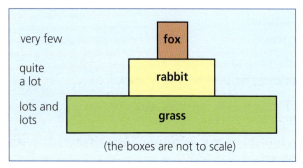

A pyramid of numbers

Cover the page. Can you remember what producers and consumers are? Check your answer.

Biomass

Sometimes a pyramid of numbers does not give a true picture of what is happening in a food chain. We need to look at the mass of living material (**biomass**) in a community. A **pyramid of biomass** nearly always gives a good idea of what is being transferred up a food chain.

For example, in the pyramid of numbers on the left, the tree is a single organism. Many caterpillars feed on the tree. But the pyramid of biomass on the right gives you a better idea of how much energy the tree supplies.

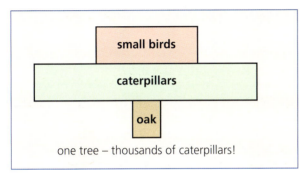

A pyramid of numbers	*A pyramid of biomass*

At each stage in a food chain, material and energy are lost (in the waste left by the consumers). The biomass of the organisms gets less as you go along the food chain.

The more stages there are in a food chain, the more biomass is lost.

This means that food production is more efficient if we have shorter food chains. For example, humans eating cereal grain is more efficient than feeding grain to cattle so humans can eat the meat. Put another way, if it takes 100 sacks of grain to produce enough beef to feed a family of four people, think how many more families could be fed if they ate the grain themselves!

Questions

1 In the garden you see blackbirds eating slugs. The slugs feed on plants. Draw a simple food chain to show this.   *Plants → slugs → blackbirds*

2 In a river plants are fed on by fish, which in turn are eaten by larger fish. Construct a pyramid of biomass to show this.

Eating waste

All living things remove materials from their surroundings. They need these materials so they can carry out their life processes (such as growth, reproduction and respiration). In doing these things, they produce waste. When they die and decay, these materials are returned to the surroundings.

Waste from organisms includes:

■ parts that are discarded, such as leaves from trees

■ products of excretion such as urine

■ undigested food, which passes through the digestive system, such as faeces

■ dead bodies.

microorganisms break down faeces and dead bodies. These microorganisms could be bacteria or fungi. The process is known as **decay**.

Microorganisms work faster if it is warm and wet with plenty of oxygen. They use waste as food to release energy for themselves.

How do we use microorganisms?

We use microorganisms in two ways:

■ to break down plants in compost heaps

■ to break down sewage on sewage farms.

The process of decay releases substances that plants use to grow. We use the products of compost heaps to fertilise (add nutrients to) our gardens.

The products of the breakdown of sewage can also be used as fertiliser.

If this **recycling** of materials did not take place then, very soon, all of the Earth's materials would be used up.

If a community of organisms takes in and uses as many materials as it releases through decay, the community is said to be **stable**.

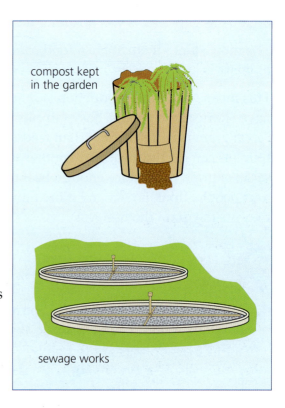

compost kept in the garden

sewage works

The carbon cycle

One important material that is recycled is carbon. This diagram shows how it is used and then recycled to the air ready to be used again.

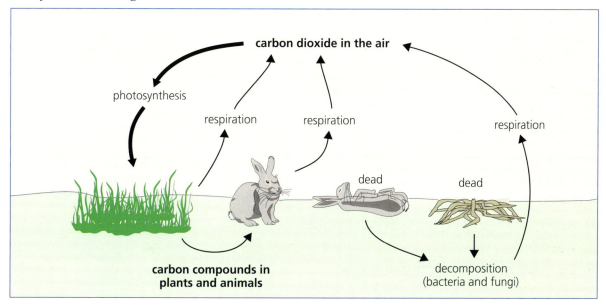

carbon dioxide in the air

photosynthesis

respiration   respiration   respiration

dead   dead

carbon compounds in plants and animals

decomposition (bacteria and fungi)

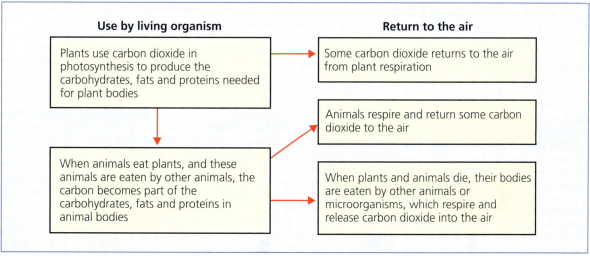

Use by living organism	Return to the air
Plants use carbon dioxide in photosynthesis to produce the carbohydrates, fats and proteins needed for plant bodies	Some carbon dioxide returns to the air from plant respiration
	Animals respire and return some carbon dioxide to the air
When animals eat plants, and these animals are eaten by other animals, the carbon becomes part of the carbohydrates, fats and proteins in animal bodies	When plants and animals die, their bodies are eaten by other animals or microorganisms, which respire and release carbon dioxide into the air

Questions

1 This question is about the carbon cycle. Copy and complete the sentences using these words:

   ~~carbon dioxide~~   **fungi**   **oxygen**   **decay**   ~~respiration~~   ~~bacteria~~

   When a plant dies _fungi_ and _bacteria_ break the plant down. They use up _oxygen_ and release _carbon dioxide_ as the process of _decay_ is brought about by _respiration_

2 Give **two** ways in which humans use microorganisms.

   Sewage work.
   Compost plant

How do humans affect the environment?

Up to about 200 years ago the human population on Earth was so small the effect of human activities was small and localised. But the population has grown rapidly since then and is changing the environment in a number of ways. Humans use up land that could be used by other plants and animals. We do this by:

- building
- dumping our rubbish
- farming to feed the world
- getting raw materials (quarrying).

The things that humans do may pollute the environment. We pollute:

- water – with sewage, fertilisers and poisonous chemicals
- air – with smoke and poisonous gases
- land – with poisonous chemicals such as pesticides and herbicides (weedkillers), which are then washed into lakes and rivers.

When we burn fossil fuels (that is coal, oil and gas) carbon dioxide and other gases are released into the atmosphere. The gases sulphur dioxide and nitrogen oxides can dissolve in rain to make it acidic. This is called **acid rain**. Acid rain can damage trees. If it makes rivers and lakes too acidic it can kill other plants and animals.

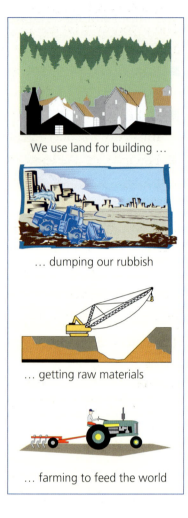

We use land for building …

… dumping our rubbish

… getting raw materials

… farming to feed the world

Are things getting worse?

Yes they are! When the human population was much smaller, human activity only had a small overall effect on the Earth. But there are now many more humans. There is more industry. Many of us enjoy a better way of life that uses up more energy (for example, electricity, cars). This means:

- the Earth's raw materials (including non-renewable fossil fuels) are being used up more quickly
- we produce more waste – unless we deal with it properly it will cause more and pollution.

Cover the page, then write down how acid rain is formed. Check your answer.

Non-renewable raw materials include coal. **Renewable** raw materials include wood.

Greenhouse Effect

Forests are being cut down. This is called **deforestation**. The wood may be used for timber and the land for agriculture. This has several results.

■ If the wood is burned then carbon dioxide is released as a product of combustion.

■ If the wood is left to decay then the respiring microorganisms release carbon dioxide.

■ Fewer trees use less carbon dioxide to photosynthesise so less carbon is 'locked up' in wood and the carbon cycle is disturbed.

Carbon dioxide in the atmosphere is also released by the burning of fossils fuels (for example, coal for power stations, petrol from oil).

Methane gas is released into the atmosphere by cattle farming and by rice fields.

The levels of these two gases are rising. They act like a blanket, trapping some of the Sun's energy, which would normally be reflected back out of our atmosphere. So the temperature of the Earth increases. This is known as the 'Greenhouse Effect'.

A rise in temperature of a few degrees Celsius may cause:

■ significant changes in the Earth's climate

■ a rise in the level of the sea.

All the issues described on these pages are environmental problems that everyone must face. We must find ways of balancing the needs of the world's growing population with the need to protect our planet for future generations. This is called **sustainable development**.

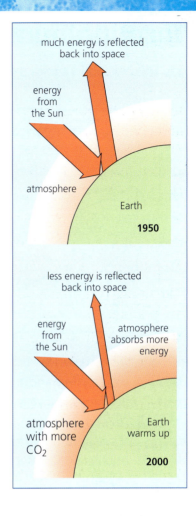

much energy is reflected
back into space

energy
from
the Sun

atmosphere

Earth

1950

less energy is reflected
back into space

energy
from
the Sun

atmosphere
absorbs more
energy

atmosphere
with more
CO_2

Earth
warms up

2000

Questions

1 Write down **three** ways in which the land available for wildlife has been reduced over the last 200 years.

2 You are travelling in the family car. How is the car helping to produce more acid rain?

3 There is more carbon dioxide in our atmosphere now than there was 100 years ago. Why do scientists believe that this will cause the atmosphere to become warmer?

Terminal exam questions

1 This is a food web for a wood.

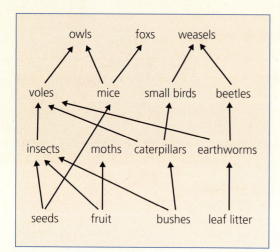

a i Name **two** physical factors that would affect the amount of fruit produced in a year. [2]

ii Name **two** factors (different from those above) that would affect the population of caterpillars in the wood. [2]

b i In one year the caterpillar population is very low. What is likely to happen to the population of small birds? Explain your answer. [2]

ii If the mouse population is low, what effect is this likely to have on the vole population? Explain your answer. [2]

[8 marks]

2 a i In what form do plants take up carbon from the atmosphere? [1]

ii Give **two** different uses of carbon in a plant. [2]

b Suggest and explain **two** different ways that carbon in a plant may be recycled to the atmosphere. [4]

c Name **two** ways in which humans use microorganisms. [2]

[9 marks]

3 a i Suggest **two** reasons for pollution being an increasing problem on the planet. [2]

ii Suggest **two** reasons for the amount of land available to plants and animals becoming less and less. [2]

b State **three** ways in which humans are polluting the planet. [3]

[7 marks]

4 This is a pyramid of numbers for a food chain in a pond.

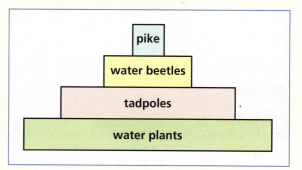

a i Which organism is the producer? [1]

ii Which organism is the top predator? [1]

iii Name **one** organism that acts as prey. [1]

b Name **two** different things the tadpoles might compete for. [2]

c This is a pyramid of numbers for a food chain that might be found in a garden.

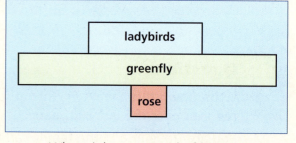

Why might a pyramid of biomass give you a better picture of what is going on? [1]

[6 marks]

Total for test: 30 marks

Why do we look like we do?

Similarities

People often look a bit like one or both of their parents. This is because male and female sex cells from their parents have joined together to form them. The sex cells pass on some of the **characteristics** of the parents' to their children.

Family members can look similar …

'Characteristics' means the way you look. For example, your height, the colour of your eyes and the shape of your nose are all characteristics.

Differences

Although children look like their parents in some ways, overall they are different. There are two reasons for this:

- Their parents' sex cells contain different combinations of characteristics (for example, eye colour and height). When they join together, this information is mixed. Each new child has a new and unique combination of characteristics.

- The conditions in which children live and grow can affect their characteristics (for example, food and living conditions affect weight and height).

All plants and animals have similarities and differences due to **inherited** characteristics and **environmental causes**, or a combination of both. For example, the size of plants may be inherited from the parent plants, but is also affected by amount of light, water and nutrients they have.

Gregor Mendel

Mendel was the first person to discover the scientific clue to the way that characteristics are inherited. In the 1850s he carried out some experiments with garden peas. By selecting and mating tall peas and short peas in different combinations, he was able to work out that these characteristics are inherited by special 'factors' we now call **genes**. It took another 100 years for scientists to discover genes and prove Mendel's **law of inheritance**.

Reproduction and variation

Genes and chromosomes

Characteristics are controlled by **genes**. The nucleus of every cell in your body contains genes carrying the plans for your body's development. Different genes control different characteristics.

The nucleus of every cell contains **chromosomes**, which are made up of many genes. Chromosomes are made from a long molecule of DNA. A gene is a section of a DNA molecule.

The chromosomes in the body cells are in pairs. When an animal or plant is growing the body cells divide to provide more cells for growth. We also need to replace cells that are destroyed or worn away.

The number of chromosome pairs in body cells is different for each type of plant or animal. Human body cells have 23 pairs, making 46 chromosomes altogether.

One pair of chromosomes carries the genes that decide the sex of a person. In females the chromosomes in the pair are the same (**XX**). In males they are different (**XY**).

Each chromosome in a pair is made up of genes that control the same characteristics (for example, a person's sex). So the genes themselves are also in pairs called **alleles**.

Sometimes the two genes in these pairs carry different information for the characteristics they both control. For example, in the pair of genes controlling someone's eye colour, there may be one allele for blue and one allele for brown.

A **dominant** allele will control the development of a characteristic. A **recessive** allele will only control this development if the dominant allele is not present. A dominant allele masks the effect of a recessive allele.

Inheriting disorders

Children can inherit disorders from their parents as well as eye colour and height. For example:

■ Huntington's chorea – this affects the nervous system. If one parent has the disorder, the child may inherit it.

■ Cystic fibrosis – this is a disorder of cell membranes. Both parents have to carry the gene for a child to inherit the disorder. If only one parent is a carrier, or if one parent has the disorder and the other is not a carrier, then none of the children will have it.

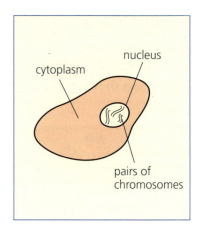

nucleus
cytoplasm
pairs of chromosomes

Chromosomes are made up of **genes**. Genes that control the same characteristic are called **alleles**. Alleles are found in pairs.

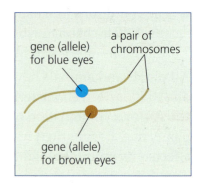

a pair of chromosomes
gene (allele) for blue eyes
gene (allele) for brown eyes

A **carrier** is someone whose cells carry a gene for a particular disorder, but the person does not show signs of the disorder itself.

■ Sickle cell anaemia – this is a disorder of red blood cells. The cells cannot carry so much oxygen. The allele for sickle cell anaemia is recessive. Carriers of the disorder can be at an advantage in countries where malaria is present.

Sexual reproduction

In body cells, chromosomes are found in pairs. On these chromosomes pairs of genes (alleles) control the same characteristic. In sex cells, however, there is only one allele from each pair. This is because there is only one chromosome from each pair.

In **sexual reproduction** a male sex cell and a female sex cell join together. Sex cells are also called **gametes** (in humans these are the sperm and egg). The offspring are all different. Another way of putting this is to say that they vary, and so these differences are known as **variation**.

In the sex cells, just as other body cells:
● the nucleus controls the cell
● chromosomes are in the nucleus
● each gene controls a characteristic.

Asexual reproduction

There are no sex cells involved at all in **asexual reproduction**. It is really reproduction by growth. For example, if you plant one daffodil bulb then several years later there will be a number of bulbs. The new bulbs grow from the original one. There are now more bulbs than when you started, so reproduction has taken place.

The new bulbs are exact copies of the parent, with exactly the same genes. We call them **clones**.

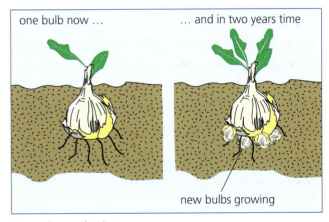

one bulb now … … and in two years time

new bulbs growing

Asexual reproduction

Questions

1 Copy and complete the sentences, using words from this list:

chromosomes   alleles   nucleus   genes

The genetic material in human cells is found in the _____ . In each human body cell there are 23 pairs of _____ , which are made up of _____ . These are also found in pairs and sometimes carry different information for the same characteristic. These are known as _____ .

2 Why is a clone the same as its parent?

3 The petals of a flower may be either red or white. A plant with red flowers is crossed with a plant with white flowers. All of the resulting seeds grow into plants with flowers with red petals. Which gene is dominant, the gene for red petals or the gene for white petals?

Controlling breeding

Breeding the animals and plants we want

We may grow a particularly pretty red rose. How do we get another one? It's simple – we take a cutting and it will grow into a plant exactly like the parent.

Both cuttings and other forms of asexual reproduction are forms of **cloning**. The parents and their offspring are genetically identical.

A cutting needs warm, wet conditions for the new roots to grow well.

Modern cloning techniques

These include:

- **Tissue culture** – growing new plants from part of a plant. Small groups of cells can be used for this.

- **Embryo transplants** – splitting apart a developing embryo before the cells become specialised, to make identical embryos. These are placed in the wombs of (or **transplanted** into) host mothers and become new, genetically identical individuals.

Dolly the sheep made headline news in 1997. She was the first animal to be cloned from adult cells. She is an identical copy of her genetic mother, but has no father!

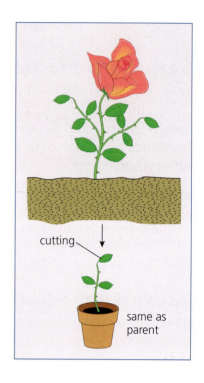

cutting

same as parent

Selective breeding

What if we want a fast horse? You can't just cut a piece off and grow it! You have to breed together a fast male horse and fast female horse. Hopefully the foal will also be fast. This is known as **selective breeding**.

We do this with many animals and plants. For example, we selectively breed:

- cows to produce more milk
- pigs to produce leaner bacon
- wheat to produce more seed
- peaches to produce sweeter fruit.

However, if we carry on selecting only some characteristics of a species to suit our needs, some alleles will be lost from the population forever. These alleles will no longer be available for selective breeding, and we will not be able to produce new varieties when conditions change.

Cover the page, then write down what is meant by 'selective breeding'.
Check your answer.

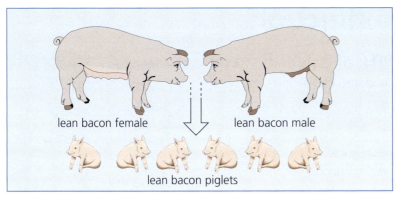

Selective breeding of pigs

Genetic engineering

Useful genes can be 'cut out' of chromosomes. They can be transferred to bacteria and they will continue to make the same protein. By doing this on a large scale, useful amounts of the protein can be made. Human insulin is now produced this way and it helps those suffering from diabetes a great deal.

What do you think?

There are many advantages to cloning and genetic engineering. Producing pest-resistant crops and cows that produce more milk makes economic sense for farmers, and helps feed people in poorer countries. Genetically modified (GM) plants can be resistant to disease so no insecticides are necessary.

But are GM foods safe to eat? What effects do they have on the environment? If we can clone sheep, what about cloning humans? Would this be morally right? Who decides what sort of people are 'desirable' and 'not desirable'?

Scientists, politicians and we the public have to look at all the advantages and disadvantages when deciding what is the best way to use these new techniques.

Questions

1 What conditions are necessary for a cutting to grow new roots properly?
2 What do we call the sections cut out of the chromosomes in genetic engineering? What are the sections used for?
3 What is a clone?

Evolution and extinction

How do species develop?

We know that some species that existed thousands or millions of years ago have died out because we have found their remains in rocks as **fossils**.
Fossils are formed:

■ from the hard parts of plants and animals (bits that do not decay easily)

■ from other parts that did not decay, for example because there was no oxygen (for the bacteria to use)

■ when parts of the animal or plant were replaced by other materials as they decayed

■ when traces of animals or plants are preserved, such as footprints.

Fossils give us a picture of how species have changed (**evolved**) over millions of years. We know that all living things on the planet today have come from organisms that first developed over three billion years ago. These were very simple life forms. This is called the **theory of evolution**

The diagram shows how the horse has evolved.

A **species** is a group of one sort of organism. For example, lions are a species.

This fossil is formed from the hard parts (skeleton) of a fish that decayed least

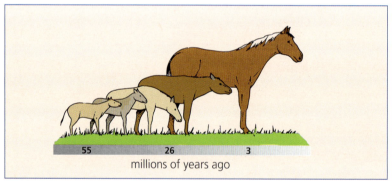

55   26   3
millions of years ago

Evolution of the horse

Natural selection · · · · · · · · · · · · · · · ·

Evolution occurs through a process called **natural selection**. It works like this:

■ There is a wide variation between members of the same species.

■ Predation, disease and competition from other species (for example, for food) will cause large numbers to die.

■ Those individuals best suited to survive these problems will breed.

Cover the page, then write down how fossils may be formed.
Check your answer.

■ The genes that have enabled these individuals to survive will be passed on to their offspring.

■ The new generation is better suited to survive these pressures from their environment.

An example of evolution can be seen today. Antibiotics are used to help cure humans of infections caused by bacteria. Some bacteria survive these antibiotics and breed. This means that over a period of time bacteria become resistant to the antibiotics, and so the antibiotics are no longer useful for fighting infection.

How do species die?

Species need to be able to adapt to changes. For example:

■ their environment may change (for example, it gets warmer or colder on the planet)

■ new predators may evolve, or new diseases, that can kill them

■ another species may evolve that competes with them (for example, for food).

If evolution does not occur so species can adapt to survive these changes, they will eventually become extinct.

How do new species begin?

Sometimes when conditions change a new species develops from an existing one.

A change in members of the species might be caused by a **mutation**. This is a change in the genes of an organism. Mutations occur naturally. However, there is more chance of a mutation if an organism is exposed to:

■ ionising radiation (for example, ultraviolet light, X-rays)

■ radioactive substances

■ some chemicals.

The more you are exposed to these things, the greater the chance of a mutation.

Charles Darwin
Charles Darwin was a scientist in the 1800s whose book *The Origin of Species* caused a big upset! He collected fossils and studied many living species, to show that evolution occurs through lots of tiny changes (**natural selection**). Through natural selection, new species can evolve. For example, humans have evolved from apes.

It took a long time for his ideas to be accepted, because they went against the teachings of the Church at that time. Many people believed that humans were the ancestors of Adam, who was created 'ready made' as a man by God.

Questions

1 What is a mutation?

2 State **three** things that might cause a species to die out.

3 State **two** possible causes of a mutation.

4 Why are there changes in a species over a long time?

Controlling human reproduction

We often want to control our own reproduction, but not for selective breeding purposes! We do it to avoid having babies, or to increase the chances of having them.

One way of doing both is for women to control their **fertility**. Fertility means the ability to reproduce. A woman's fertility is controlled by hormones in her body that:

- release an egg from her ovaries every month
- make the lining of her womb thicker to receive the egg if it is fertilised.

These hormones are produced (secreted) by the pituitary gland in her brain and by the ovaries themselves.

Hormones that are produced artificially can be used to stop the woman's ovaries producing eggs. This is how the **oral contraceptive** (birth control pill) works. It is the most reliable method of contraception but, for a few women, can produce unpleasant side-effects. These include giddiness, nausea or, very occasionally, thrombosis (blood clots).

If a woman's ovaries are not releasing an egg every month she may find it difficult to conceive a child when she does want one. Other artificially produced hormones can stimulate the release of eggs from her ovaries. These are fertility drugs.

Hormones are chemical messengers in the body.

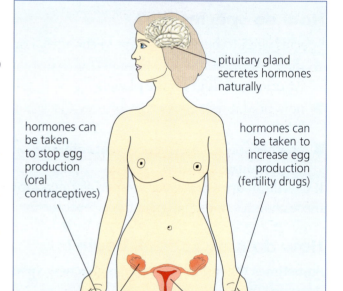

hormones can be taken to stop egg production (oral contraceptives)

pituitary gland secretes hormones naturally

hormones can be taken to increase egg production (fertility drugs)

womb

ovary

Hormones control fertility in women

Questions

1. Copy and complete the sentences using these words:

   fertility   hormones   pituitary gland   secreted

   The ability of a woman to have a child is controlled by chemical messengers called _____ . This ability is known as the woman's _____ . The chemical messengers are produced by the _____ . Another word for produced is _____ .

2. Women who cannot produce eggs can be given fertility treatment. Suggest advantages and disadvantages of this treatment.

Terminal exam questions

1 a Copy and complete the following sentences. Use words from this list to fill spaces 1–4:

alleles
chromosomes
genes
nucleus

The ____1____ controls the cell. Within this part of the human cell are pairs of ____2____. These are made up of ____3____, which control characteristics such as eye colour. They may be found in two different forms called ____4____, for example, blue and brown eye colour. [4]

b i Why do gardeners take cuttings? [1]
ii Sometimes the new plants are not identical to the parent. Suggest **one** reason for this. [1]
iii Name **two** conditions necessary for cuttings to grow well. [2]
[8 marks]

2 a i Which part of a cell does cystic fibrosis affect? [1]
ii How is the disease inherited? [2]
b i Name **one** symptom of Huntington's chorea. [1]
ii How is this disease inherited? [2]
[6 marks]

3 a What is a gene? [2]
b What is an allele? [2]
c What is the difference between a recessive gene and a dominant gene? [2]
[6 marks]

4 a i What is meant by the term 'selective breeding'? [2]
ii Why is selective breeding carried out? [2]

b How do hormones help in:
i birth control [2]
ii fertility treatment? [2]
[8 marks]

5 This strawberry plant is producing new strawberry plants.

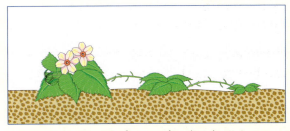

a What type of reproduction is taking place? [1]
b Why will all of the new strawberry plants be the same as the parent strawberry plant? [2]
c How would you go about breeding a new strawberry plant that develops bigger strawberries? [2]
[5 marks]

Total for test: 33 marks

Materials and their properties

Metals

Earth materials

Patterns of chemical change

Structures and bonding

The periodic table

All of the elements are arranged in rows, in order of their relative atomic masses. Elements in the same columns have similar properties. Elements in the same column are known as a **Group**. The whole arrangement is known as the **periodic table**.

Examples of metals include:

- potassium in Group 1

- calcium in Group 2.

Li lithium	Be beryllium	
Na sodium	Mg magnesium	
K potassium	Ca calcium	Transition metals
Rb rubidium	Sr strontium	
Cs caesium	Ba barium	
Fr francium	Ra radium	

There are a few elements that do not fit this pattern. For example, argon has a greater atomic mass than potassium but because of its properties it is better placed before potassium in the table. So argon is placed in Group 0.

More than three-quarters of all elements are metals. In the periodic table most metals are found:

- in the two left-hand columns (Groups 1 and 2)

- in the central block (transition metals)

Group 1 metals

The elements in Group 1 are known as the **alkali metals**. They get this name because they form hydroxides that dissolve in water to form alkaline solutions.

The alkali metals:

- have a low density (the first three are less dense than water and will float as they react)

- react with non-metals to form ionic compounds. These compounds will then dissolve in water to form colourless solutions. For example:

potassium + oxygen ⟶ potassium oxide

- react with water to give off hydrogen. For example:

sodium + water ⟶ sodium hydroxide + hydrogen

- react with water to form hydroxides that dissolve in the water to form alkaline solutions (such as sodium hydroxide in the equation above) .

Transition metals

In the centre of the periodic table is another block of metallic elements. These are the **transition metals**. These metals include copper and iron.

Like all metals, the transition metals:

■ are good conductors of heat

■ are good conductors of electricity

■ can easily be bent or hammered into different shapes.

However, they are different to the alkali metals in Group 1. Transition metals:

■ have high melting points (all except for mercury, which has a low melting point and is a liquid even at room temperature)

■ are much harder, tougher and stronger

■ are not nearly as reactive as the alkali metals so they do not react (corrode) as quickly with either water or oxygen.

These properties make transition metals very useful. For example:

■ **iron** is very useful for making structures, such as girders in buildings or in bridges. It is usually used in the form of steel.

■ **copper** is very useful for making things, which either transfer heat (such as the bottoms of pans for cooking) or transfer electricity (such as wires).

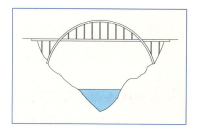

Most of the transition metals form coloured compounds. These compounds can be seen:

■ in the coloured glazes on pottery

■ when copper has been weathered (it turns green).

Some transition metals, for example iron and **platinum** are used as catalysts (chemicals that speed up reactions).

Questions

1   Copy and complete the three equations using these words:

oxygen   hydrogen   hydroxide   hydrochloric

magnesium + _____ ⟶ magnesium oxide

calcium + water ⟶ calcium _____ + hydrogen

zinc + _____ acid ⟶ zinc chloride + _____

2   Give **three** differences between the alkali metals and the transition metals.

Extracting metals from their ores

Reactivity of metals

The more reactive a metal, the faster it will react with:

- air (producing metal oxides)
- water (to produce metal hydroxides and steam)
- dilute acid (to produce metal salts and hydrogen).

By comparing the reactions of different metals, we can work out a **reactivity series**.

Some metals in order of their reactivity:

potassium (K)	**most**
sodium (Na)	**reactive**
calcium (Ca)	
magnesium (Mg)	
aluminium (Al)	
carbon (C)	
zinc (Zn)	
iron (Fe)	
tin (Sb)	
lead (Pb)	
copper (Cu)	
silver (Ag)	**least**
gold (Au)	**reactive**

Metal ores

Most metals are found in the Earth's crust in compounds with other elements (for example, metal oxides). They are often mixed up with other compounds in the rocks as well. Before we can use these metals they have to be separated from other elements. This may be done chemically.

Any rock that contains enough of a metal or its compounds to make it worth extracting is called an **ore**.

Extracting metals

Gold is an unreactive metal. It is found in the Earth as a metal itself. Chemical separation is not needed, unlike for other metals from their ores.

If a metal is found as a metal oxide the oxygen has to be removed to leave the metal behind. This removal of oxygen is called **reduction**. It can be done by using a more reactive substance to displace or 'bully' the metal out of its compound.

We can use the idea of reactivity series to extract metals from their ores. A more reactive metal (higher up in the reactivity series) can displace a less reactive metal (lower down in the reactivity series) from its compounds.

Carbon is more reactive than iron so we can use it to take the oxygen from the iron in the iron oxide found in the ore.

Carbon is not a metal, but we include it in the reactivity series because it behaves like a metal in a way that makes it useful for extracting other metals from their ores.

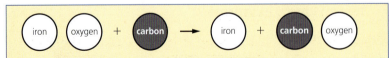

Carbon removes the oxygen from the iron

You need to heat the substances before the reaction will work. This is done in a **blast furnace**.

Extracting iron

Iron is extracted in a blast furnace like this:

1 Iron ore (haematite), coke (carbon) and limestone are put into the reaction chamber. These are the solid raw materials.

2 Hot air is blasted into the furnace. The coke burns to give off carbon dioxide:

carbon + oxygen ⟶ carbon dioxide

3 This reaction gives off lots of energy. In the heat, the carbon dioxide reacts with more coke to make carbon monoxide:

carbon dioxide + carbon ⟶ carbon monoxide

4 The carbon monoxide reduces the iron oxide in the iron ore. Iron and oxygen are produced:

■ The molten (melted) iron flows to the bottom of the furnace.

■ The oxygen reacts with carbon monoxide to produce carbon dioxide. This is called **oxidation**.

iron oxide + carbon monoxide ⟶ iron + carbon dioxide

5 Limestone (which was added with the raw materials) helps remove acidic impurities from the molten iron at the bottom of the furnace by reacting with them. This produces slag, which floats on the pure molten iron. The slag is run off as a waste product.

6 The pure molten iron flows out of the bottom of the furnace.

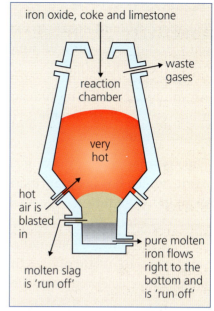

The blast furnace

Oxidation – removal of oxygen
Reduction – addition of oxygen

Questions

1 Which of these metals, lead, tin or magnesium cannot be extracted from its oxide by carbon? Explain why.

2 Copy and complete the sentences, using words from this list:

> less   reduce   iron   more
> slag   carbon monoxide   calcium carbonate

Carbon can _____ iron oxide to _____ as carbon is _____ reactive than iron. In fact, it is actually _____ that reacts with iron. Limestone (_____) is added to react with any impurities and form _____ .

Extracting aluminium

The most difficult metals to extract are the most reactive ones, because it is difficult for other elements to push them out of their compounds.

Aluminium is much more reactive than iron. It is also more reactive than carbon, so carbon cannot be used to reduce aluminium.

The raw material for making aluminium is aluminium oxide, which has been purified from aluminium ore (bauxite). Aluminium is extracted from its ore (aluminium oxide) by **electrolysis**. Aluminium oxide is made up of positive aluminium ions and negative oxygen ions. When substances are made of **ions** they can be broken down by passing an electric current through them.

The substance has to be molten (melted) or dissolved before this will work. Why? So that the ions are free to move.

The least reactive metals (for example, gold) are found just as the metals, not in compounds.

During electrolysis:

■ the positive aluminium ions move to the negative electrode

■ the negative oxygen ions move to the positive electrode.

Electrolysis is used to extract most reactive metals from their ores. The pure metals are always formed at the negative electrode and a gas is often given off at the positive electrode.

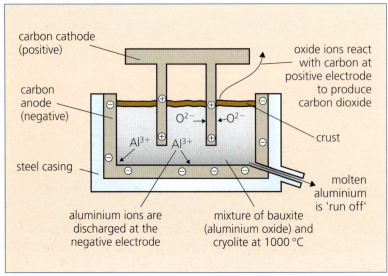

carbon cathode (positive)

oxide ions react with carbon at positive electrode to produce carbon dioxide

carbon anode (negative)

$O^{2-} \rightarrow$ $\leftarrow O^{2-}$

Al^{3+} Al^{3+}

crust

steel casing

molten aluminium is 'run off'

aluminium ions are discharged at the negative electrode

mixture of bauxite (aluminium oxide) and cryolite at 1000 °C

The extraction of aluminium

How does the process work?

Aluminium oxide has a very high melting point, but it can be dissolved in molten cryolite at a much lower temperature. This saves the manufacturers lots of money because they use less energy to heat the ore.

The electrodes are made of carbon. Aluminium forms at the negative electrode. Oxygen forms at the positive electrode – this makes the electrode burn away quickly so it has to be replaced often.

Purifying copper

Very pure copper is needed for electricity wires. We get it by purifying impure copper using electrolysis.

A positive electrode made of impure copper is dipped in a solution of copper sulphate. Positive copper ions move to the negative electrode and pure copper collects there.

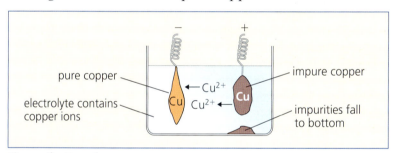

The purification of copper

Questions

1 This question is about the electrolysis of aluminium. Copy and complete the sentences using these words:

   negative   oxide   positive   cryolite

   The ore of aluminium is aluminium _____ . It has a high melting point so is added to molten _____ . The aluminium ions are deposited at the _____ electrode and the oxygen ions move to the _____ electrode.

2 Why do substances have to be dissolved or melted if they are going to be electrolysed?

3 Using information from pages 46–49 place these three elements in a reactivity series:

   aluminium (Al)   carbon (C)   iron (Fe)

   From other knowledge you have of chemistry now add sodium (Na) and gold (Au) to your reactivity series.

Corrosion

The metals we extract from ores have many uses. We don't want them turning back into metal oxides (oxidising or corroding). There are ways of preventing metals doing this.

Iron (or steel) corrodes more quickly than most other transition metals. It reacts with oxygen in the air. This is also called **rusting**.

| iron + oxygen ⟶ iron oxide |

You can help to prevent iron rusting by:

■ connecting it to a more reactive metal (for example, zinc or magnesium). This is called **sacrificial protection**.

■ mixing it with another metal (for example, chromium) to make an alloy (stainless steel) that does not corrode.

Aluminium does not corrode as quickly as you would expect from its position high up in the reactivity series. This is because the outside of the metal reacts with oxygen to make a thin film of aluminium oxide. This quickly covers the rest of the aluminium, so air and water can no longer get to it.

Aluminium is a useful structural metal and can be mixed with other metals (for example, magnesium) to make it harder, stronger and stiffer.

Making metal compounds

Neutralisation

Substances can dissolve in water to produce solutions that are acidic, alkaline or neutral.

Alkali metals (in Group 1 of the periodic table) have oxides and hydroxides that dissolve in water to form alkaline solutions. These react with acidic solutions in neutralisation reactions. The metal compounds produced this way are called salts.

| acid + alkali ⟶ salt + water |

In a neutralisation reaction, **indicators** are used to tell you when the reaction is complete. The salt solution is neutral.

The salt produced in a neutralisation reaction depends on:

■ the metal in the alkali

■ the acid used.

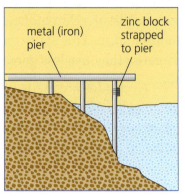

The zinc block prevents the iron pier from rusting

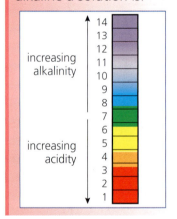

The pH scale is used to show how acidic or alkaline a solution is:

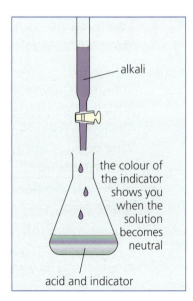

Neutralising hydrochloric acid produces chlorides:

$$\text{hydrochloric acid} + \text{sodium hydroxide} \longrightarrow \text{sodium chloride} + \text{water}$$

Neutralising nitric acid produces nitrates:

$$\text{nitric acid} + \text{sodium hydroxide} \longrightarrow \text{sodium nitrate} + \text{water}$$

Neutralising sulphuric acid produces sulphates:

$$\text{sulphuric acid} + \text{sodium hydroxide} \longrightarrow \text{sodium sulphate} + \text{water}$$

> Sodium chloride is a salt. It is also called 'salt'. There are many other salts (for example, potassium nitrate and calcium sulphate). So salt is not the only salt!

Ammonia dissolves in water to form an alkaline solution (ammonium hydroxide). This can also be neutralised to form an ammonium salt.

Bases

Unlike the alkali metals, transition metals have oxides and hydroxides that do not dissolve in water. They are called **bases**.

> Hydrogen ions (H^+) make acidic solutions.
> Hydroxide ions (OH^-) make alkaline solutions.

$$\text{acid} + \text{base} \longrightarrow \text{salt} + \text{water}$$

A transition metal salt can be made by reacting a base with an acid.

You can produce a solution of a soluble transition metal salt like this:

1. the insoluble metal oxide or hydroxide is added to the acid
2. until no more will react
3. the excess metal oxide or hydroxide is then filtered off.

Questions

1 This question is about neutralisation reactions. Copy and complete the table, using these words:

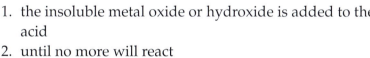

potassium nitrate   sodium nitrate   potassium sulphate   calcium chloride

Acid	Alkali	Products
sulphuric acid	+ potassium hydroxide	⟶ + water
nitric acid	+ potassium hydroxide	⟶ + water
hydrochloric acid	+ calcium hydroxide	⟶ + water
nitric acid	+ sodium hydroxide	⟶ + water

2 Which ion is present in all acids?

Module test questions

1 This question is about the pH scale.
Match words from the list with the labels 1–4 on the diagram.

4 **weak alkali**
2 **weak acid**
3 **neutral**
1 **strong acid**

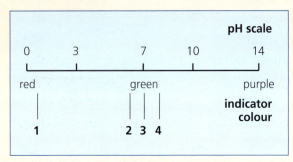

2 This question is about the different types of chemical reaction.

Match words from the list with each of numbers 1–4 in the table.

4 **displacement**
3 **reduction**
1 **neutralisation**
2 **oxidation**

	Description
1	the reaction between an acid and an alkali
2	when a metal oxide loses its oxygen
3	when a metal becomes a metal oxide
4	when a more reactive metal removes a less reactive metal from a compound

3 This table is about the reactions of some metals.

Choose words from the list for each of the numbers 1–4 in the table.

2 **metal oxide**
1 **metal chloride**
4 **hydrogen**
3 **metal hydroxide or oxide**

	Reaction
1	the result of the reaction between a metal and hydrochloric acid
2	the result of the reaction between a metal and oxygen
3	the gas given off when a metal reacts with hydrochloric acid
4	the result of a reaction between metal and water

4 This question is about the reactivities of different elements.

Match words from the list with spaces 1–4.
gold 4 **aluminium** 1
carbon 2 **iron** 3

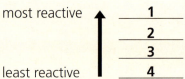

5 In the electrolysis of aluminium oxide (bauxite), which **two** of the following statements are correct?

A cryolite is used to reduce the melting point of the ore
B the positive electrode is made of aluminium
C oxygen forms at the negative electrode
D negative ions gain an electron to form an atom
E aluminium forms at the negative electrode

6 When hydrochloric acid and sodium hydroxide react together the **two** products are:

A sodium chloride
B hydrogen
C carbon dioxide
D sodium sulphate
E water.

7 This is a picture of a blast furnace.

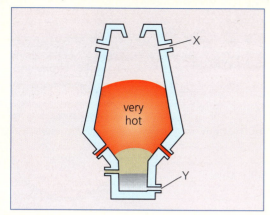

1. What happens at X?

   A waste gases are given off
   B molten iron flows
   C molten slag is run off
   D hot air is blasted in.

2. What happens at Y?

   A waste gases are given off
   B molten iron flows
   C molten slag is run off
   D hot air is blasted in.

3. Which substance is formed first when coke burns in the furnace?

   A carbon
   B carbon dioxide
   C slag
   D carbon monoxide.

4. The substance that reduces the iron is:

   A carbon dioxide
   B limestone
   C carbon monoxide
   D carbon.

8 When compared to alkali (Group 1) metals which of these statements are true of transition metals?

   A they mostly have higher melting points
   B they are softer
   C they react less quickly
   D they are less strong
   E they form compounds that are not as coloured.

9 These sentences are about the uses of some metals. Use words from the list to fill in the spaces 1–4 in the sentences.

   A **a good conductor of electricity**
   B **strong**
   C **strong with a low density**
   D **easily shaped**

Iron is used to build bridges because it is
____**1**____ .
Copper is used in electric wiring because it is ____**2**____ and to make water pipes because it is ____**3**____ .
Aluminium is used in the manufacture of aeroplanes because it is ____**4**____ .

The structure of the Earth

How the Earth is formed

The Earth is nearly a sphere (a ball shape). It has a layered structure, which includes:

- a thin crust
- a very viscous mantle (very thick liquid), which goes almost half way to the Earth's centre
- a core in the centre, containing nickel and iron – the outer part is liquid and the inner part solid.

The rocks that make up the Earth's crust are not as dense as the Earth as a whole. This means that the inside of the Earth must be made of different materials, which are more dense than the crust.

The Earth's surface is made of continental crust and oceanic crust. The rocks in continental crust are described as 'granitic'. They are slightly less dense than the oceanic rocks, which are described as 'basaltic'. This means that the continental crust rises above the ocean bed, forming dry land above sea level.

The crust of the Earth is continually moving. This causes changes that include some mountains being formed and others being worn away.

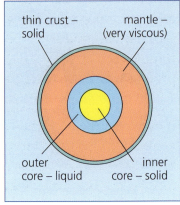

thin crust – solid   mantle – (very viscous)

outer core – liquid   inner core – solid

The structure of the Earth

Movement of the Earth's crust results in the **rock cycle**, which takes place continuously but is very slow.

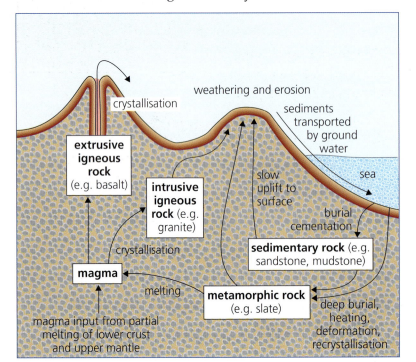

crystallisation

weathering and erosion

sediments transported by ground water

extrusive igneous rock (e.g. basalt)

intrusive igneous rock (e.g. granite)

slow uplift to surface

sea

burial cementation

crystallisation

sedimentary rock (e.g. sandstone, mudstone)

magma

melting

metamorphic rock (e.g. slate)

deep burial, heating, deformation, recrystallisation

magma input from partial melting of lower crust and upper mantle

The rock cycle

Sedimentary rocks

These were formed from layers of sediment (such as sand, mud or the shells of dead shellfish) deposited on top of one another. The weight squeezes out the water and sediment becomes cemented together, with other fragments, by salts crystallising out of the water. The process often takes millions of years.

Geologists can study sedimentary rocks to find out how they were formed. For example, if different sediments were deposited at different times the rocks will be layered; or rocks may have ripple marks that show they were formed by currents or waves.

Sedimentary rocks, on the surface, usually lie on top of older rocks. These rock layers can be:

- tilted
- folded
- fractured (faults)
- and sometimes turned upside down!

These movements are caused by very large forces. Large-scale Earth movements can, over a long time, cause mountain ranges to form. These replace older mountains that have been worn down (eroded) by the weather.

Sedimentary rocks include:

- **sandstone** – made of grains of sand
- **limestone** – made from calcium carbonate (often from shell remains of living organisms).

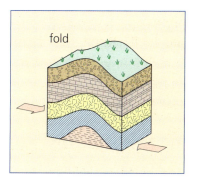

fold

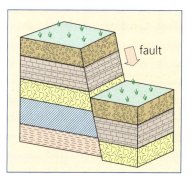

fault

Metamorphic rocks

These are often found in present day and old mountain ranges. They are formed when there is high temperature and pressure, often caused by the mountain building process.

Metamorphic rocks are igneous or sedimentary rocks that have been buried underground by the Earth's movements. They become compressed and heated. Their texture may change without the rock melting.

Metamorphic rocks include:

- **marble** – formed in this way from limestone
- **slate** – formed mainly from mudstone
- **schist** – rocks composed of bands of interlocking crystals.

Questions

1   How is sedimentary rock formed?
2   How can sedimentary and igneous rocks become metamorphic rocks?

Earth movements

The pattern of continents

The edges of continents are sometimes separated by thousands of kilometres of ocean. It seems that their shapes could fit together quite well (for example, South America and Africa). They also seem to have similar patterns of rocks and fossils. This suggests that they were once joined together and over millions of years have moved apart.

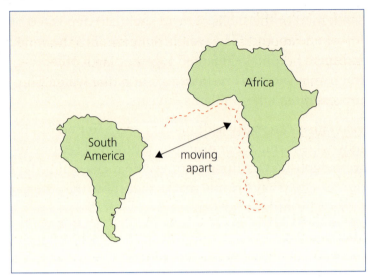

These continents are moving apart

Tectonic plates

The Earth's crust and the upper part of the mantle are called the lithosphere. It is split into a number of very large pieces – rather like a jigsaw. These pieces are called **tectonic plates**, which 'float' on the mantle underneath.

The plates are moving by a few centimetres every year because of convection currents in the mantle. The energy for this comes from heat released by radioactive processes inside the Earth.

We now know that mountains have been formed when plates have collided with each other, forcing one of the plates upwards.

Do not try to remember this map!

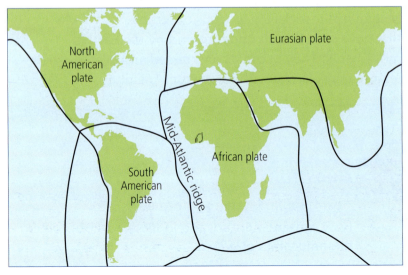

Tectonic plates

It used to be believed that as the Earth cooled its circumference became smaller, and that this 'shrinking' forced rocks upwards.

Wegener first put forward the theories of continental drift caused by the movement of tectonic plates. However, it was not until 50 years after his death that his theories were accepted.

Earthquakes and volcanoes

Tectonic plates are always moving and this means that they are constantly pushing against each other. Sometimes as two plates push against each other very high pressures are created. At a certain point the pressure will be so great that one plate will go under another or slip past the other plate. As there has been such a lot of pressure this happens quickly and causes an Earthquake. No-one can predict when this will happen as no-one knows when the pressure will be great enough to cause the sudden movement. When one plate is pushed underneath another, the rock goes down into the Earth. The rock melts and becomes **magma**. This magma is under great pressure and can be forced back up through the crust to become a volcano.

Igneous rock is formed when magma cools. If magma cools quickly on the surface (for example, from a volcano) it forms extrusive igneous rock with small crystals (for example, basalt).

If magma forms slowly below the crust it forms **intrusive** igneous rock with larger crystals (for example, granite).

volcano
erupts

D

C molten
rock forced
up

Tectonic plate

Tectonic
plate

A plate
forced down

Mantle

B rock melts
(very high pressure)

A volcano

Questions

1 Why do we think that the continents are moving apart?

2 What causes the tectonic plates to move?

Materials from the Earth

Limestone

Limestone, a sedimentary rock, is mainly calcium carbonate. It can be quarried and used as a building material. Powdered limestone can be used to neutralise acidity in lakes and soils.

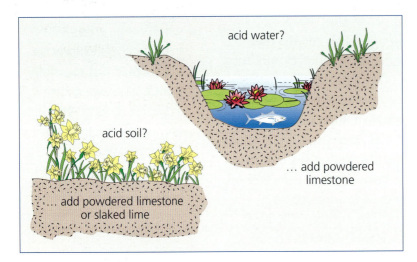

acid water?

acid soil?

... add powdered limestone

... add powdered limestone or slaked lime

If you heat limestone in a kiln it breaks down into **quicklime** (calcium oxide) and carbon dioxide. This type of reaction is called thermal decomposition. Quicklime reacts with water to produce **slaked lime** (calcium hydroxide). This reduces soil acidity.

Cement is made by roasting powdered limestone with powdered clay in a rotary kiln. If it is mixed with water, sand and crushed rock a slow chemical reaction produces a hard, stone-like building material called **concrete**.

Glass is made by heating a mixture of limestone, sand and soda (sodium carbonate).

glass vase made from limestone, sand and soda

Crude oil and its products

Crude oil is obtained from the Earth's crust. It was formed from the remains of organisms that lived millions of years ago. Crude oil, like coal and natural gas, is a **fossil fuel**.

Crude oil is a mixture of very many compounds. A mixture is made up of two or more elements or compounds that are not chemically combined together. This means that mixtures can be separated by physical processes such as dissolving and filtration.

Crude oil and natural gas were produced as a result of heat and pressure (in the absence of air) acting on the remains of animals and plants trapped in sedimentary rock. This process took millions of years.

Separating crude oil ● ● ● ●

Oil is separated by **distillation** – it is heated and then the gases that come off are cooled so that they turn back into liquids.

Most of the compounds in oil are made up of hydrogen and carbon only, and so are called **hydrocarbons**. These different hydrocarbons can be separated by evaporating the oil, then condensing the gases that evaporate at different temperatures. A different **fraction** comes off at each temperature. Each fraction consists of a type of hydrocarbon that has molecules with a similar number of carbon atoms. This is known as **fractional distillation**.

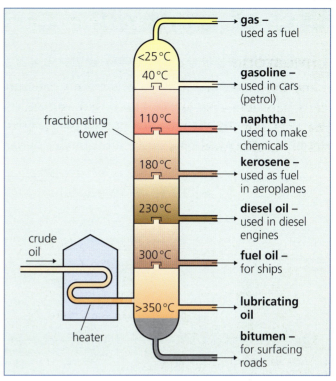

Fractional distilation of crude oil

Hydrocarbon molecules in crude oil vary a great deal in size. The larger the molecule (which means it has more carbon atoms) the:

- ■ higher the boiling point
- ■ less volatile it is (this means it is more difficult to evaporate)
- ■ less easily it flows (this means it is more viscous)
- ■ less easy it is to ignite (this means it is less flammable).

This means that hydrocarbons with large molecules are not very useful as fuels.

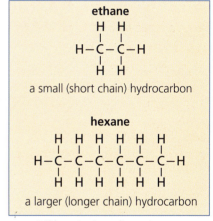

Two different hydrocarbons

Questions

1 This question is about limestone. Copy and complete the sentences using these words:

   calcium carbonate   cement   slaked lime   quicklime

   Limestone is mainly _____ . When it is heated _____ is produced (calcium oxide). This can be reacted with water to produce _____ (calcium hydroxide). If you roast powdered limestone with powdered clay then you have made _____ .

2 How does the length of the carbon chain affect the boiling point of a hydrocarbon?

Uses of crude oil

Larger hydrocarbons can be broken down into smaller, more useful hydrocarbons. This is called **cracking**.

The hydrocarbons are heated until they vapourise (turn into gas). The vapours are then passed over a hot catalyst until the molecules break down into smaller hydrocarbon molecules.

A catalyst is a substance that speeds up a chemical reaction

$$\boxed{\text{7C}} \quad H-\underset{\underset{H}{|}}{\overset{\overset{H}{|}}{C}}-\underset{\underset{H}{|}}{\overset{\overset{H}{|}}{C}}-\underset{\underset{H}{|}}{\overset{\overset{H}{|}}{C}}-\underset{\underset{H}{|}}{\overset{\overset{H}{|}}{C}}-\underset{\underset{H}{|}}{\overset{\overset{H}{|}}{C}}-\underset{\underset{H}{|}}{\overset{\overset{H}{|}}{C}}-\underset{\underset{H}{|}}{\overset{\overset{H}{|}}{C}}-H$$

'cracked' into

$$\boxed{\text{4C}} \quad H-\underset{\underset{H}{|}}{\overset{\overset{H}{|}}{C}}-\underset{\underset{H}{|}}{\overset{\overset{H}{|}}{C}}-\underset{\underset{H}{|}}{\overset{\overset{H}{|}}{C}}-\underset{\underset{H}{|}}{\overset{\overset{H}{|}}{C}}-H \quad + \quad \boxed{\text{3C}} \quad \overset{H}{\underset{H}{\diagup}}C=\underset{\underset{H}{|}}{\overset{\overset{H}{|}}{C}}-\underset{\underset{H}{|}}{\overset{\overset{H}{|}}{C}}-H$$

more useful substances

'Cracking' a hydrocarbon

Products from cracking can be used as fuels and as plastics.

Plastics

Plastics are polymers (long chains of the same small molecule joined together). Examples include:

■ poly(ethene) – used for making plastic bags and bottles
■ poly(propene) – used for making crates and ropes.

Most plastics cannot be broken down (decomposed) by microorganisms. They are described as **non-biodegradable**. This means that when thrown away and dumped on waste disposal sites, they do not rot down with the other rubbish. Carbon is 'locked up' in the plastics, so cannot be used again by plants and animals as part of the natural carbon cycle.

The carbon cycle is covered in more detail in the Module *Environment* (see page 29).

Fuels

Fuels are burned in air (oxygen) to release the energy needed for many activities. For example, the petrol we put in cars, much of the electricity we use around the home and the gas we use in our camping stoves all come originally from crude oil.

These fuels contain carbon and hydrogen, and some also contain sulphur. When they burn, the gases produced include:

- carbon dioxide
- water (vapour), which is an oxide of hydrogen
- sulphur dioxide.

> Nitrogen oxides are also produced when fuels are burned.

These gases are released into the atmosphere, where they cause pollution such as the Greenhouse Effect and acid rain.

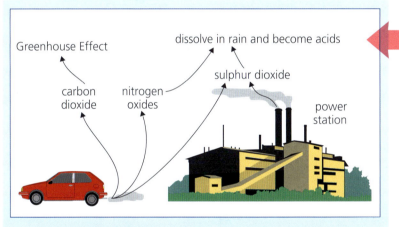

> The Greenhouse Effect and acid rain are covered in more detail in the Module *Environment* (see pages 30–31).

The **Greenhouse Effect** is caused by too much carbon dioxide in the atmosphere. It acts like the roof of a greenhouse over the Earth, letting energy from the Sun in but not letting the heat from the Earth out. As a result, the Earth gets warmer.

Acid rain is produced from acidic gases such as sulphur dioxide dissolving in rainwater. When this collects in rivers and ponds, organisms can die because of the increased acidity of the water.

Questions

1. How are large hydrocarbons 'cracked' into smaller hydrocarbons?
2. When fuels burn carbon and hydrogen oxides are produced. What is the common name for hydrogen oxide?

The Earth's atmosphere

The atmosphere was formed over millions of years, but it has taken only a hundred years or so of human activity to disturb the natural balance of the atmosphere. Before we can understand the effects we are having on the Earth's atmosphere, we need to understand how it was formed.

How the atmosphere was formed

For the last 200 million years the atmosphere has been made up of the following gases:

- about 80% nitrogen
- about 20% oxygen
- small amount of carbon dioxide
- small amounts of water vapour
- small amounts of other gases, such as the 'noble' gases.

This is very different to the Earth's atmosphere 1 billion years ago. Then it was more like the atmosphere on Venus today. The atmosphere then was formed by a lot of volcanic activity. It contained:

- mainly carbon dioxide
- some water vapour
- some methane and ammonia
- little or no oxygen.

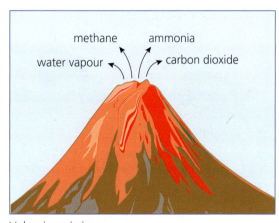

Volcanic emissions

As the Earth cooled, the water vapour formed the oceans.

As plants evolved and their numbers increased on the Earth, the atmosphere started to change.

- As they photosynthesised, they 'polluted' the atmosphere with oxygen.
- The methane and ammonia in the atmosphere reacted with the oxygen, producing carbon dioxide and nitrogen.
- Most of the carbon from the carbon dioxide became 'locked up' in sedimentary rocks as carbonates and fossil fuels.

These changes in the atmosphere had two main effects:

- The original microorganisms could not tolerate the oxygen in the atmosphere, so died out.
- New organisms that could photosynthesise and respire were able to evolve and survive.

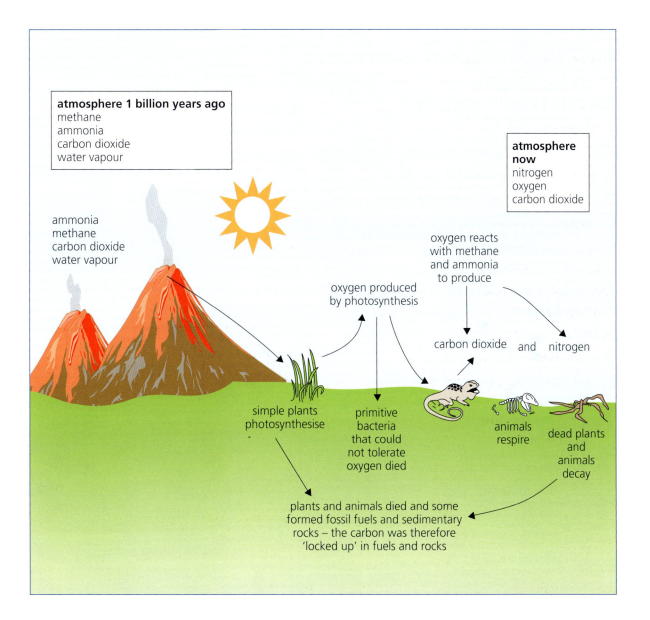

atmosphere 1 billion years ago
methane
ammonia
carbon dioxide
water vapour

atmosphere now
nitrogen
oxygen
carbon dioxide

ammonia
methane
carbon dioxide
water vapour

oxygen reacts with methane and ammonia to produce

oxygen produced by photosynthesis

carbon dioxide   and   nitrogen

simple plants photosynthesise

primitive bacteria that could not tolerate oxygen died

animals respire

dead plants and animals decay

plants and animals died and some formed fossil fuels and sedimentary rocks – the carbon was therefore 'locked up' in fuels and rocks

Questions

1 Which **four** gases were present in the Earth's original atmosphere?
2 Why is there nitrogen in the Earth's atmosphere now?

Module test questions

1 The table gives some information about four materials.

Match words from the list with the numbers 1–4 in the table.

concrete
slaked lime
quicklime
calcium carbonate

	Information about the material
1	made by a chemical reaction between cement and other materials
2	the main chemical in limestone
3	produced when you heat (roast) limestone
4	made by adding calcium oxide and water together

2 This question is about the uses of some materials found in crude oil.

Match words from the list with numbers 1–4 in the table.

bitumen
fuel oil
gasoline (petrol)
kerosene

	The use of the material
1	used to surface roads
2	used as a fuel for cars
3	used as a fuel in aeroplanes
4	used as a fuel in ships

3 This question is about some of the gases in our atmosphere.

Match words from the list with numbers 1–4 in the table.

carbon dioxide
sulphur dioxide
oxygen
nitrogen

	Information about the gas
1	This gas represents about 20% of the atmosphere
2	This gas causes the Greenhouse Effect
3	This gas helps to cause acid rain
4	This gas represents about 80% of the atmosphere

4 Which **two** of the following are heated with sand to make glass?

    A quicklime
    B soda
    C limestone
    D slaked lime
    E clay.

5 Which **two** of the following are true of large hydrocarbons when compared to smaller hydrocarbons?
Larger hydrocarbons:

    A have a higher melting point
    B flow very easily (less viscous)
    C are easier to evaporate
    D are more reactive
    E are less easy to ignite (burn less easily).

6 When the Earth was formed, which **two** of the following statements about the atmosphere were true?

The atmosphere contained:

    A a lot of water vapour
    B very little carbon dioxide
    C a lot of oxygen
    D no methane
    E some ammonia.

7 This is a diagram of the structure of the Earth.

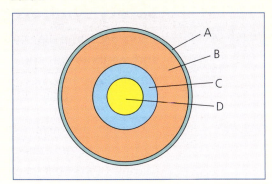

1. Which letter represents the crust?

   A   B   C   D

2. Which letter represents the mantle?

   A   B   C   D

3. Which letter represents the part of the Earth likely to be the most dense?

   A   B   C   D

4. Which letter represents the area where convection currents are taking place? (These currents cause the movement of the Earth's plates.)

   A   B   C   D

8 This is a diagram of a volcano erupting.

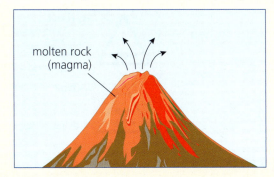

molten rock (magma)

1. An example of molten rock that could come from the volcano would be:

   A   sandstone
   B   limestone
   C   basalt
   D   marble.

2. If the rock cools slowly below the Earth's surface it is:

   A   extrusive igneous rock with small crystals
   B   extrusive igneous rock with large crystals
   C   intrusive igneous rock with small crystals
   D   intrusive igneous rock with large crystals.

3. Magma on the Earth's surface can become sedimentary rock if it:

   A   becomes buried and erupts again onto the surface
   B   wears away and is put under heat and pressure
   C   becomes buried, melts to form magma, then cools below the surface
   D   wears away and the grains become cemented together.

4. An example of an intrusive igneous rock is:

   A   marble
   B   sandstone
   C   mudstone
   D   granite.

In the laboratory

Speeding up chemical reactions

You can increase the speed chemicals react with each other by doing any of these things:

■ increasing temperature

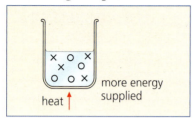

■ increasing the concentration of the reacting chemicals

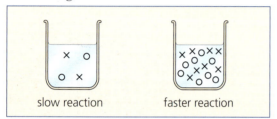

■ increasing the surface area of one of the reacting chemicals (by cutting it into smaller pieces)

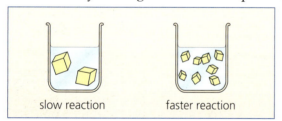

■ increasing the pressure on the reacting chemicals (when these are gases).

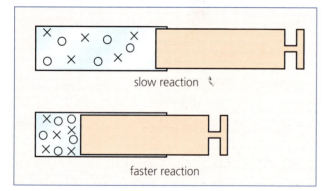

■ using a **catalyst**. A catalyst speeds up a reaction but is not used up itself. It can be used over and over again. Different reactions need different catalysts.

The speed of a reaction is called the **rate of reaction**.

Safety symbols

There are some diagrams and symbols that you should be able to recognise in an examination.

You must also be able to name one hazardous (dangerous) substance (for example, sulphuric acid).

oxidising
provide oxygen that allows other materials to burn more fiercely

highly flammable
catch fire easily

toxic
can cause death when swallowed or breathed in or absorbed through the skin

harmful
similar to toxic substances but less dangerous

corrosive
attack and destroy living tissues including eyes and skin

irritant
not corrosive but can cause reddening or blistering of the skin

Cover the page, then write down the different ways of increasing the rate (speed) of a reaction. Check your answer.

Chemicals react only when the particles bump into each other (collide) with enough energy. The minimum amount of energy you need to start a reaction is called the **activation energy**.

Increasing the temperature, concentration or pressure on reacting chemicals means they collide more often and with more energy. This is why the reaction speeds up.

In industry, increasing the rate of reaction is important because it can reduce costs and increase profits.

Cover the page, then write down what is meant by 'activation energy'.
Check your answer.

Has the reaction been speeded up?

You can measure the rate of reaction in different ways. You can:

■ measure the rate at which products are formed (for example, the amount of gas given off)

■ measure how fast the reacting chemicals are used up.

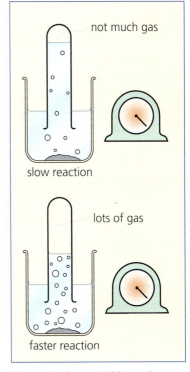

not much gas

slow reaction

lots of gas

faster reaction

Measuring how quickly products are produced

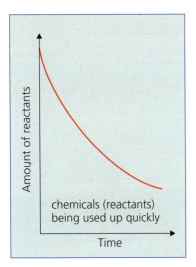

chemicals (reactants) being used up quickly

Measuring how quickly reactants are used up

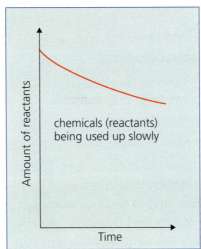

chemicals (reactants) being used up slowly

Questions

1 Why does increasing the concentration of reacting chemicals increase the rate of reaction?

2 Copy and complete the sentences, choosing words from this list:

   increase   greater   collide   decrease   less

   You may _increase_ the rate of a reaction if you increase the temperature. This is because the particles _collide_ more often and with _greater_ energy.

3 How might you tell that a reaction has speeded up?

Using living organisms

Living cells use chemical reactions to produce new materials. Humans use yeast and bacteria to produce substances that they want.

Yeast cells convert (change) sugar into carbon dioxide and alcohol.

This process is called fermentation and it is used:
- to produce alcohol in wine and beer
- to produce carbon dioxide bubbles to make bread rise.

Bacteria are used to make yoghurt from milk. They change the lactose sugar in the milk into lactic acid.

These reactions take place faster when it is warm but not hot. Living organisms use enzymes as catalysts. Enzymes are proteins, which are usually damaged by temperatures above about 45 °C. Different enzymes work best at different pH values. We can use enzymes too, to speed up chemical reactions.

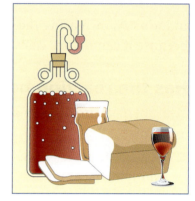

Products using fermentation

The uses of enzymes

Enzymes are used in everyday processes from washing clothes to making foods.

Biological detergents (washing powders) may contain:
- protein-digesting enzymes (**proteases**)
- fat-digesting enzymes (**lipases**).

These enzymes digest foods that have got onto clothes. The clothes must be washed at a low temperature otherwise the enzymes would denature (lose their shape) and not work. This low temperature saves heat energy and therefore money.

A number of different foods are made by industry with the help of enzymes.

- Proteins in some baby foods are pre-digested by proteases to help the baby complete the digestion.
- Starch syrup can be digested into more useful sugar syrup using **carbohydrases**.
- Glucose syrup can be converted into fructose syrup, which is much sweeter and therefore less needs to be used in some foods, which helps in dieting. The enzyme used in this process is an **isomerase**.

Enzymes are used in industry to bring about reactions at normal temperatures and pressure. Without enzymes, these reactions would need expensive equipment that uses a lot of energy, which adds to manufacturing costs.

The advantages of using microorganisms and enzymes to bring about chemical reactions are obvious – they enable reactions to take place more easily and this saves money.

Disadvantages are less obvious. Any microorganisms and enzymes need to be tested rigorously to make sure they are safe to use, for example in foods or items that come into contact with the skin. Carrying out trials takes time and costs money, which manufacturers have to consider in their overall costings.

Do chemical reactions release energy?

The answer is that some do and some don't.

An **exothermic** reaction releases energy, often as heat, which will warm up the surroundings. This happens when you burn a fuel.

> When fuel burns energy is released as heat.

> **Exothermic** – heat given off.
> **Endothermic** – heat taken in.

An **endothermic** reaction results in energy, often as heat, being taken from the surroundings.
A reversible reaction can take place in either direction. This means that if it is exothermic in one direction it must be endothermic in the other direction. The same amount of energy will be transferred in each direction.

| hydrated copper + (heat energy) sulphate (blue) | $\rightleftharpoons$ | anhydrous copper + water sulphate (white) |

> This reaction is used the other way round as a test for water.

Reversible reactions are chemical reactions in which the products of the reaction will react to produce the substance(s) that you started with. They can be written like this:

$A + B \rightleftharpoons C + D$

For example:

| ammonium chloride (white solid) | $\rightleftharpoons$ | ammonia + hydrogen chloride (both are colourless gases) |

> Cover the page, then write down what you understand by the word 'exothermic'. Check your answer.

Questions

1 State **two** different foods made by industry that involve the use of enzymes.

2 Why do enzymes make a reaction go faster at 30 °C and stop working at 45 °C?

3 Yeast is very useful to humans. Draw a spider diagram to show **three** useful substances that yeast helps us make. Put **yeast** at the centre of your diagram.

Chemical calculations

These are easy when you know how! To work out what is happening in chemical reactions we need to know the masses of the chemicals involved. We work this out by using **relative atomic masses** (A_r).

You will find relative atomic masses in the data book in the exam. These make it possible to work out the **relative formula mass** (M_r) of a compound.

Atoms of different elements have different relative atomic masses. For example:

$^{39}_{19}$K potassium $^{35}_{17}$Cl chlorine
$A_r = 39$ $A_r = 35$

> To work out M_r – add up all of the relative atomic masses in a compound.

You must be able to calculate the relative formula mass (M_r) of a compound if you are given its formula.

Worked example

Q What is the M_r of carbon dioxide (CO_2)?

A The relative atomic mass of carbon is 12
the relative atomic mass of oxygen is 16

A_r of carbon = 12
A_r of oxygen = 32   (there are two and each
                        has a mass of 16)
          $M_r = 44$

Worked example

Q What is the M_r of sulphuric acid (H_2SO_4)?

A The relative atomic mass of hydrogen is 1
the relative atomic mass of oxygen is 16
the relative atomic mass of sulphur is 32

A_r of hydrogen = 2   (there are two and each has
                        a mass of 1)
A_r of sulphur = 32
A_r of oxygen = 64   (there are four and each has
                        a mass of 16)
          $M_r = 98$

> The relative atomic mass (A_r) is the top number. For example, $^{16}_{8}$O – the relative atomic mass is 16.

Worked example

Q What is the percentage of carbon in carbon dioxide (CO_2)?

A M_r of carbon dioxide $= 44$
   A_r of carbon $= 12$

   % of carbon $= \dfrac{12}{44} \times 100$

   $= 27.3\%$

You must also be able to work out the percentage of an element in a compound.

Worked example

Q Work out the percentage of nitrogen in nitric acid (HNO_3)

A Work out the relative formula mass (M_r) of nitric acid first.
   A_r of hydrogen $=$ 1
   A_r of nitrogen $= 14$
   A_r of oxygen $= 48$ (there are three oxygens
             each with a mass of 16)
   $M_r = 63$
   the percentage
   of nitrogen $= \dfrac{14}{63} \times 100$

   $= 22.2\%$

Questions

1 Work out the relative formula mass (M_r) for each of these compounds:

   a calcium carbonate ($CaCO_3$)

   b magnesium sulphate ($MgSO_4$)

2 What is the percentage of:

   a sodium in sodium chloride ($NaCl$)

   b sulphur in sulphur dioxide (SO_2)?

Relative atomic masses (A_r)	
carbon (C)	12
calcium (Ca)	40
chlorine (Cl)	35
magnesium (Mg)	24
sodium (Na)	23
oxygen (O)	16

The production of fertiliser

Air is almost 80% nitrogen. This can be used to make several important chemicals including some fertilisers.

Fertilisers replace the nutrients plants take up from the soil, so farmers can grow more crops. Sometimes these fertilisers cause problems because they get washed out of the soil into rivers, ponds and lakes when it rains. Some get into our drinking water.

Ammonium nitrate fertiliser is made in the following way:

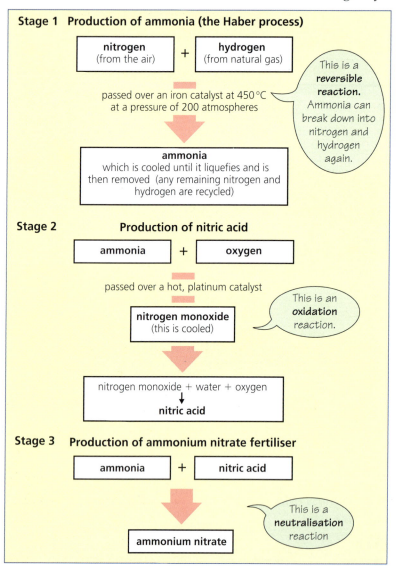

Stage 1   Production of ammonia (the Haber process)

| nitrogen (from the air) | + | hydrogen (from natural gas) |

passed over an iron catalyst at 450 °C at a pressure of 200 atmospheres

This is a reversible reaction. Ammonia can break down into nitrogen and hydrogen again.

ammonia which is cooled until it liquefies and is then removed (any remaining nitrogen and hydrogen are recycled)

Stage 2   Production of nitric acid

| ammonia | + | oxygen |

passed over a hot, platinum catalyst

This is an oxidation reaction.

nitrogen monoxide (this is cooled)

nitrogen monoxide + water + oxygen
↓
nitric acid

Stage 3   Production of ammonium nitrate fertiliser

| ammonia | + | nitric acid |

This is a neutralisation reaction

ammonium nitrate

The use of fertiliser
Nitrate fertiliser is very useful as it replaces the nitrogen taken from the soil as crops grow. However, when it gets into our drinking water it can be a health hazard, for example causing 'blue baby syndrome' in young babies. This is when the blood is not able to carry enough oxygen around the body, leading eventually to brain damage and death. Fertilisers are therefore useful but the amounts used must be managed carefully.

Questions

1   Name the **two** catalysts needed in the production of ammonium nitrate.

Terminal exam questions

1 a Humans use yeast to produce new substances. Name **two** new substances humans produce using yeast. [2]

b Bacteria are used to convert milk into yogurt. What substance in the milk is changed by the bacteria and what new substance is produced. [2]

c Both of the processes above must not be carried out above 45 °C. Why not? [2]

[6 marks]

2 a Suggest **three** ways of increasing the rate of a chemical reaction. For each one explain why it speeds up the reaction. [9]

b What is meant by the term 'activation energy'? [2]

[11 marks]

3 a i Copy and complete the following sentences about the production of ammonium nitrate. Use words from the list to fill spaces 1–4.

nitric acid
hydrogen
oxygen
nitrogen

The gases ____1____ and ____2____ are reacted together to produce ammonia. This ammonia is now reacted with ____3____ to produce nitrogen dioxide. Nitrogen dioxide is reacted with oxygen and water to produce ____4____. This product is now reacted with the ammonia to produce ammonium nitrate. [4]

ii At what temperature and pressure is ammonia produced? [2]

iii What catalyst is used for the reaction? [1]

b What problem can ammonium nitrate cause in the environment? [4]

c What is meant by the term 'endothermic reaction'? [2]

[13 marks]

4 a You will need the following information to answer this question.

Relative atomic masses (A_r)	
hydrogen	1
oxygen	16
carbon	12
calcium	40

What are the relative formula masses (M_r) of:

ii ethanoic acid, CH_3COOH [4]

iii calcium hydroxide, $Ca(OH)_2$? [4]

b What is the percentage of:

i oxygen in water, H_2O [3]

ii carbon in calcium carbonate, $CaCO_3$? [3]

[14 marks]

Total for test: 44 marks

Solids, liquids and gases

When a substance gains or loses energy, it may change its state (solid, liquid or gas).

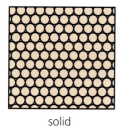
solid

liquid

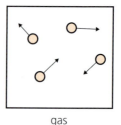
gas

You will already have learned about the three states of matter and what happens to particles during melting and evaporating. You need to remember this, but will not be tested on it at GCSE.

If a solid is heated it gains energy. The particles vibrate more and more, until they separate and become free to move. The temperature when this happens is the **melting point**. The solid becomes a liquid.

If a liquid is heated, the particles gain even more energy and move around more quickly. When they have enough energy to overcome the forces that attract the particles to each other, they escape from the liquid and become a gas. This is **evaporation**.

The temperature at which a liquid boils is called the **boiling point**.

Atoms

All substances are made of atoms. There are about 100 different sorts of atoms. A substance that contains atoms of only one sort (for example, all sodium atoms) is called an **element**.

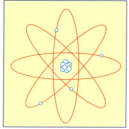

Atoms have a small nucleus. The nucleus contains protons and neutrons. Whizzing around the nucleus are electrons.

	Mass	Charge
proton	1	+1 (positive)
neutron	1	0 (neutral)
electron	almost 0	−1 (negative)

Atoms have no overall charge (they are neutral). They have the same number of protons and electrons.

Eighteenth century chemists knew that substances were made of different elements, but the idea that elements were made of atoms was not proved. Early in the nineteenth century John Dalton studied the way in which the different elements combine with one another to form chemical compounds. He argued that if elements were made of atoms, they would combine in definite proportions to produce particular substances. He tested this idea and was able to show that, for example, water is a compound made of two parts hydrogen to one part oxygen. He called this smallest unit of a chemical substance a 'molecule'. His measurements were the proof that chemists needed that atoms and molecules are the building blocks of all matter.

Protons and neutrons

All atoms of the same element have the same number of protons. For example:

- all sodium atoms have 11 protons
- all oxygen atoms have 8 protons
- all chlorine atoms have 17 protons.

Different elements have different numbers of protons. For example, only sodium has 11 protons – no other element.

The number of protons is the **proton number** (or the **atomic number**).

The number of protons plus the number of neutrons is the **mass number**.

Every element has a symbol (for example, Na is the symbol for sodium). When you write it down, you can also put the mass number at the top and the atomic or proton number at the bottom of the symbol. For example:

$$\text{mass number} \rightarrow \quad ^{23}_{11}\text{Na} \text{ (sodium)}$$
$$\text{proton number} \rightarrow$$

Isotopes

Atoms of the same element may have different numbers of neutrons. These atoms are called **isotopes** of that element.

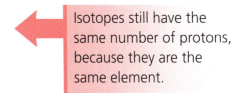

Isotopes still have the same number of protons, because they are the same element.

Questions

1 If you know the number of protons in an atom, you also know the number of electrons. Why?

2 If an element has an isotope, does the isotope have a different number of protons, neutrons or electrons?

Electrons

The electrons are whizzing around the nucleus of an atom in 'orbits'. These 'orbits' are different energy levels, sometimes called **electron shells**.

The shell closest to the nucleus is at the lowest energy level. This means that the electrons here need less energy to stay in orbit than those in any other shells. The further away from the nucleus, the higher the energy level. The electrons in any atom are always found as close as possible to the nucleus.

The first shell (nearest to the nucleus) holds a maximum of two electrons.

The next shells can hold up to eight electrons each.

You can write down an atom's **electronic structure**. For example, sodium has 11 electrons arranged like this: sodium 2, 8, 1.

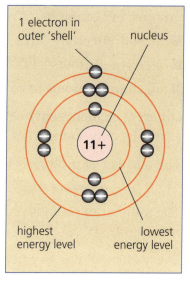

Electronic structure of sodium

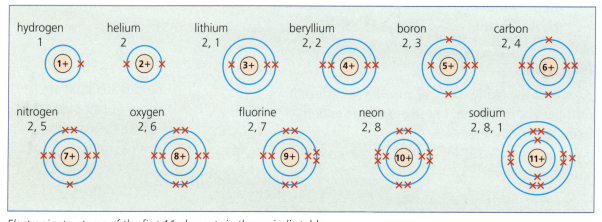

Electronic structures of the first 11 elements in the periodic table

Compounds and chemical bonds

Most substances are compounds formed from two or more atoms that are chemically combined. These are held together with chemical bonds. Chemical bonds between elements are formed in two ways:

- **ionic** bonds – the atoms give and take electrons into their outer shells (that is in the highest occupied energy levels)

- **covalent** bonds – atoms share these 'outer' electrons.

Ionic bonds

An ionic bond forms when one of the atoms in a compound gains one or more electrons, and another atom loses one or more electrons. The atoms now have a charge and are called ions. The compound is an ionic compound.

An ionic compound is a giant structure of ions. These compounds have high melting and boiling points because the bonds formed are strong.

Atoms that lose electrons become positively charged ions (for example, sodium ion, Na^+). Atoms that gain electrons become negatively charged (for example, chloride ions, Cl^-). These ions now have the electronic structure of a noble gas. That is, $Na+$ is like neon (2,8) and Cl^- is like argon (2,8,8).

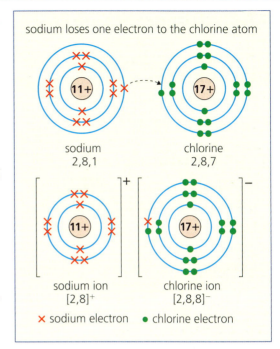

sodium loses one electron to the chlorine atom

sodium
2,8,1

chlorine
2,8,7

sodium ion
$[2,8]^+$

chlorine ion
$[2,8,8]^-$

× sodium electron   • chlorine electron

Ionic compounds are regular structures of ions called **giant ionic lattices**. Inside these structures, the forces between the oppositely charged ions are very strong. This means they have high melting points and boiling points.

When ionic compounds are melted or dissolved in water, they conduct electricity. This is because the ions are free to move around.

Metals consist of giant structures. The electrons in the outer shell of the metal atom move around through the whole structure. This means that these free-moving electrons:

■ hold the atoms of the metal together in a regular structure

■ allow the atoms to slide over one another

■ allow the metal to conduct heat and electricity.

Questions

1 Magnesium is shown as: $^{24}_{12}Mg$

   a What is its proton number?   **c** How many electrons are there?

   b What is its mass number?   **d** What is the electronic structure of magnesium?

2 Oxygen has an electronic structure of 2, 6. Draw a diagram of how magnesium and oxygen form an ionic bond.

3 Look at the diagram on page 76. Draw a similar diagram of the electronic structures of elements 12 to 20.

More about chemical bonds

When atoms form compounds their outer electron shells become full. Atoms like to have full outer shells. They can do this by gaining or losing electrons when making ionic bonds. Atoms can also share electrons to form covalent bonds.

Covalent bonds

In covalent bonds atoms share electrons to form molecules. There are bonds between the atoms *in* a molecule but not *between* molecules. So substances made of molecules usually have low melting and boiling points, because the molecules separate very easily. Molecular compounds are often liquids or gases at room temperature.

There are different ways of showing covalent bonds. For example, for ammonia:

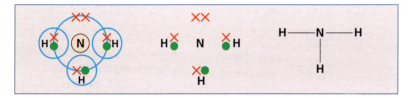

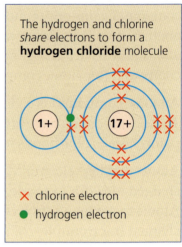

The hydrogen and chlorine *share* electrons to form a **hydrogen chloride** molecule

× chlorine electron
● hydrogen electron

A molecule of hydrogen chloride

The periodic table

You have already learned some things about the periodic table in the module **Metals** (look back at pages 44–45 to remind yourself).

In the modern periodic table the elements are arranged in order of their atomic (proton) number. This means that they are also arranged in terms of their electronic structures.

From left to right, across each row (period) of the periodic table, a particular energy level (or shell) is filled up with electrons. In the next period, the next energy level is filled up.

Families of elements with similar electronic structures (that is, the same number of electrons in their outer shells) are arranged in columns (Groups). They behave (react) in similar ways because they have similar electronic structures.

Differences in the ways elements react can also be explained by their electronic structure.

You need to be able to show the covalent bonds in:
water (H_2O)
ammonia (NH_3)
hydrogen (H_2)
hydrogen chloride (HCl)
methane (CH_4)
oxygen (O_2).

When the periodic table was first used, scientists hadn't discovered protons so didn't know about atomic numbers. They arranged the elements in order of relative atomic mass.

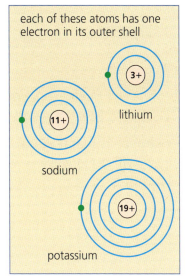

each of these atoms has one electron in its outer shell

lithium

sodium

potassium

Similar elements can be grouped

Groups													0
1	2				H				3	4	5	6	7	He
Li	Be								B	C	N	O	F	Ne
Na	Mg								Al	Si	P	S	Cl	Ar
K	Ca			transition metals									

Part of the periodic table

The history of the periodic table

For a long time chemists searched to find patterns that might explain and predict the behaviour of elements. Around 1800, John Dalton introduced the idea that chemical elements were made up of atoms, and that atoms of different elements had different masses. Thirty years later, another chemist showed that elements could be grouped into threes, or 'triads' (for example, lithium, sodium and potassium).

In 1863, John Newlands came up with the idea of arranging elements in order of their atomic masses in groups of eight, or 'octaves'. A few years later, Mendeléev published the first clear table grouping elements by their atomic masses and properties. Not all of the elements were known at the time, so this early table had gaps. When elements were eventually found that fitted the gaps, it strengthened belief in the table.

The classification of elements in this way led scientists to understand better why reactions take place. At first they just thought this information was interesting but not that useful. Now it is used to explain much of chemistry, and is an important summary of what we know about the structure of atoms.

Questions

1 Copy and complete the sentences, choosing words from this list:

   sharing   high   low   atoms   exchanging   molecule

   Two oxygen _____ join together to form an oxygen molecule (O_2). The bond is formed by _____ electrons. Oxygen is covalent. Covalent compounds tend to have _____ melting and boiling points.

2 If one element is in the same group as another in the periodic table what does this tell you?

Groups in the periodic table

Group 1 elements

These are called the **alkali metals** because when they react with water they produce an alkaline solution. They include lithium (Li), sodium (Na) and potassium (K). The alkali metals:

- have the properties of all metals
- react with non-metals to form ionic compounds – their ions carry a +1 charge (because they lose their outer electron)
- react with water giving off hydrogen and forming an hydroxide – this dissolves in the water to form an alkaline solution.

When placed in cold water, the metal floats and often moves around on the surface. The more reactive the metal, the more vigorous its reaction with water.
The further down the group the metal is:

- the lower its melting point and boiling point
- the more reactive it is.

So potassium is more reactive than sodium, which is more reactive than lithium.

A simple test for hydrogen is that it burns in air with a 'squeaky pop'.

Non-metals

About a quarter of the elements are non-metals. They are found in groups at the right-hand side of the periodic table. Group 7 and Group 0 elements have typical properties of non-metals:

- The first two Group 7 elements (fluorine and chlorine) are gases at room temperature. The third (bromine) is a liquid but vaporises at a low temperature.
- All of the Group 0 elements are gases at room temperature.
- They are brittle and crumbly when they are solid.
- Whether solid or liquid, they are poor conductors of heat and electricity (as they have no 'free' electrons in their outer shell).

Group 7 elements (the halogens)

These include fluorine (F), chlorine (Cl) and bromine (Br). The halogens:

- as gases, all have coloured vapours (chlorine is green, bromine is brown)

Cover the page. Can you remember how many electrons Group 1 metals have in their outer shell? Check your answer.

- consist of molecules that are pairs of atoms (for example, Cl_2, Br_2)
- form ionic salts in which the chloride, bromide or fluoride ion carries one negative charge, such as Na^+Br^- (sodium bromide)
- form molecular compounds with other non-metals, for example:

$$C + 2Cl_2 \rightarrow CCl_4 \text{ (tetrachloromethane)}$$

- are less reactive and have higher melting and boiling points the further down the group they are.

> Group 1 metals and Group 7 non-metals react so well together because the metal has to lose one electron (to make a full outer shell) and the non-metal has to gain one electron.

A more reactive halogen will displace a less reactive halogen from a solution of its salt in water. For example, if chlorine is added to a solution of potassium iodide then potassium chloride and iodine will result:

$$Cl_2 + 2KI \rightarrow 2KCl_2 + I_2$$

Group 0 elements (the noble gases)

These are at the very right-hand side of the periodic table. Their atoms all have full outer shells. They include helium (He), neon (Ne) and argon (Ar).

The noble gases:

- are very unreactive
- exist as single atoms (for example, Ne) and not as diatomic atoms (for example, O_2)
- are used as inert (unreactive) gases in light bulbs and electrical discharge tubes – they glow with different coloured light (you may have heard of 'neon' lights).

The first element in the group, helium, is much less dense than air and is used in balloons.

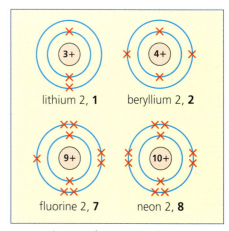

Some elements from Groups 1, 2, 7 and 0

> Noble gases are unreactive because they don't need to lose or gain electrons to get a full outer shell.

Questions

1 Give **three** properties of the halogen gases.
2 Neon has an electronic structure of 2, 8. Why is it so unreactive?
3 Why does a Group 1 element have a +1 charge when it becomes an ion?

Useful halides

The halogens (Group 7 elements) produce many useful salts. These salts are called **halides**. One of the most useful is sodium chloride.

Using sodium chloride

Sodium chloride (salt) is made when sodium and chlorine join to form an ionic compound. It is found in large amounts in the sea and underground.

The electrolysis of sodium chloride solution (brine) is an important industrial process. Sodium chloride dissolved in water produces four ions:

- positive sodium ions (Na^+) and negative chloride ions (Cl^-) from the salt (NaCl), and

- positive hydrogen ions (H^+) and negative hydroxide ions (OH^-) from the water (H_2O).

When electricity is passed through the solution:

- chloride ions (negative) move to the positive electrode, and chlorine gas is given off

- positive hydrogen ions move to the negative electrode, and hydrogen gas is given off

- a solution of sodium hydroxide (NaOH) is left behind.

> When two elements are attached by strong bonds then a lot of energy is needed to separate them.

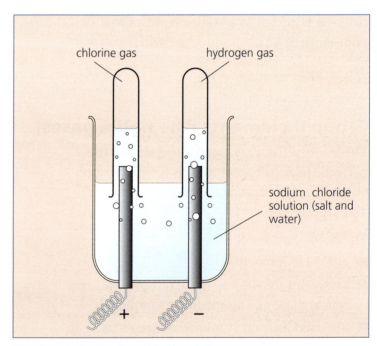

The electrolysis of sodium chloride solution

What happens at the electrodes?

Chloride ions (Cl^-) arrive at the positive electrode. An electron is lost from each chloride ion to leave it neutral again (in other words, to leave it as a chlorine atom again):

$$Cl^- - e^- \rightarrow Cl$$

But you need two chlorine atoms to make a molecule of chlorine gas, so:

$$2Cl^- - 2e^- \rightarrow Cl_2$$

This chlorine gas is given off.

> A test for chlorine is that it bleaches damp litmus paper.

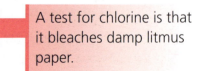

What are the substances produced used for?

- **Chlorine** is used to kill bacteria in drinking water and swimming pools – it is also used in disinfectants and bleach. The plastic PVC is a polymer made with chlorine.

- **Hydrogen** is used in the manufacture of ammonia (for fertiliser) and margarine.

- **Sodium hydroxide** is used in the manufacture of soap, paper and ceramics.

Cover the page, then write down **two** uses of chlorine and **two** uses of hydrogen.
Check your answer.

More uses for the halides

Hydrogen halides (for example, hydrogen chloride, HCl) are gases that dissolve in water to produce acidic solutions (for example, hydrochloric acid, H^+Cl^-).

Metal halides are used in the production of photographs. Silver chloride, silver bromide and silver iodide are reduced to silver by the action of light, X-rays and radiation from radioactive substances. They are used to make photographic film and photographic paper.

Questions

1 This question is about the electrolysis of sodium chloride solution. Copy and complete the sentences, using these words:

   chlorine   electron   chloride   positive

   In the electrolysis of sodium chloride negative _____ ions move to the _____ electrode. The ions then lose an _____ . The ions become atoms. Two atoms join to become a _____ molecule.

2 State **two** uses of silver halides.

3 When sodium chloride solution is electrolysed useful substances are produced. Draw a spider diagram to show these useful substances. Put **sodium chloride** at the centre of your diagram.

Symbols, formulae and equations

Chemical symbols

There are over 100 elements known to us today. They are all shown in the periodic table. The ten you are most likely to come across are listed here.

Element	Symbol
hydrogen	H
carbon	C
nitrogen	N
oxygen	O
sodium	Na

Element	Symbol
magnesium	Mg
sulphur	S
chlorine	Cl
potassium	K
calcium	Ca

Every element has its own symbol, so instead of writing out the name of the element you can use its symbol.

Formulae

Compounds are made from a number of elements. These can be shown by chemical formulae, which show the atoms in the compounds and how many of them there are. For example:

- carbon dioxide is shown as CO_2: which means that each molecule has one atom of carbon and two atoms of oxygen
- sodium chloride is NaCl: which means that for every one atom of sodium there is one of chlorine

You need to know the formulae of some other common covalent compounds. These are shown in the table.

Covalent compound	Formula
carbon dioxide	CO_2
sulphur dioxide	SO_2
ammonia	NH_3
nitrogen monoxide	NO
nitrogen dioxide	NO_2

Ionic compounds

These are compounds made up of positively and negatively charged ions. They are usually the salts of metals or hydrogen. You can work out their formulae if you know the charge on the ions.

In the exam you will be able to find the charges on all the ions you need. They are in the data book.

Worked example

Q What is the formula of the ionic compound calcium chloride?

A A calcium ion has two positive charges (Ca^{2+}) and a chloride ion has one negative charge (Cl^-).

So each calcium ion needs two chloride ions to balance its positive charges. Therefore: calcium chloride is $CaCl_2$.

Equations

Equations show us what happens in a chemical reaction. The substances at the start of a reaction (the **reactants**) are always on the left of the arrow. The substances they produce (the **products**) are on the right.

Reactions can be written as word equations and symbol equations. For example:

> sodium hydroxide + hydrochloric acid → sodium chloride + water
> $NaOH$ HCl $NaCl$ H_2O

The total mass of reactants is always the same as the total mass of products. This means that the same number of atoms of each element must be on each side of the arrow. The equations must be **balanced**.

For example, calcium metal and hydrochloric acid react to produce calcium chloride (a salt) and hydrogen:

> $Ca + HCl \rightarrow CaCl_2 + H_2$

However, the number of atoms of each element must be the same on each side of the arrow. So we write:

> $Ca + 2HCl \rightarrow CaCl_2 + H_2$

You can also add information about the **state** of each substance in a symbol equation. That is, whether they are solid, liquid, gas or dissolved in water.

> $Ca(s) + 2HCl(l) \rightarrow CaCl_2(s) + H_2(g)$

State	Symbol
solid	s
liquid	l
gas	g
aqueous solution (dissolved in water)	aq

Questions

1. Work out the formulae for the following compounds. Use the information in the table and on these pages to help you.
   a sodium hydroxide   c sodium oxide
   b magnesium oxide   d magnesium chloride.

Ion	Formula
sodium	Na^+
magnesium	Mg^{2+}
hydroxide	OH^-
oxide	O^{2-}

2. Write a word equation for each of these balanced symbol equations.
   a $2Mg + O_2 \rightarrow 2MgO$ b $2K + 2H_2O \rightarrow 2KOH + H_2$ c $2Na + Cl_2 \rightarrow 2NaCl$

3. The gas methane burns in oxygen to produce carbon dioxide and water.
   a Balance this symbol equation for the reaction.
   $CH_4 + O_2 \rightarrow CO_2 + H_2O$
   b Use the table above to help you add state symbols to the equation.

Terminal exam questions

1 Sodium can be represented as $^{23}_{11}$Na.

  a i How many protons has sodium? [1]

    ii How many electrons has sodium? [1]

   iii How many neutrons has sodium? [1]

   iv What is the atomic mass of sodium? [1]

  b Sodium has the electron structure 2, 8, 1.
Copy and complete the diagram to show this structure. [2]

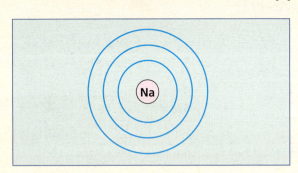

  c i Potassium (2, 8, 8, 1) reacts violently with fluorine (2, 7). Copy and complete the diagrams to show how this happens. [3]

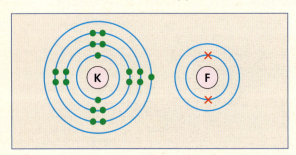

    ii What type of bond is formed? [1]

[10 marks]

2 This is part of the periodic table.

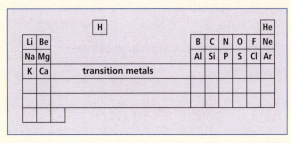

  a i Shade the Group 2 metals. [1]

    ii Name **two** of the elements shown in Group 1. [2]

   iii Name the **two** elements shown in Group 7. [2]

  b Why are the elements in Group 0 so unreactive? [2]

[7 marks]

3 a All of the elements are represented in the periodic table. Potassium is represented in this way:

$$^{39}_{19}\text{K}.$$

   i What is the atomic mass of potassium? [1]

   ii How many protons has potassium? [1]

   iii How many neutrons has potassium? [1]

  b Sodium is presented in this way:

$$^{23}_{11}\text{Na}.$$

  Draw a diagram to show the electronic structure of a sodium atom. [3]

  c Lithium has the electronic structure 2, 1 and chlorine has the structure 2, 8, 7.

   i Draw an electronic diagram to show how the two atoms react with each other to produce lithium chloride. [3]

   ii What type of bond has been formed? [1]

   iii During this reaction the lithium atom becomes an ion. What is an ion? [2]

   iv How does lithium become an ion? [2]

[14 marks]

Total for test: 31 marks

Physical processes

Energy

Electricity

Forces

Waves and radiation

The transfer of heat

There are three different ways that heat can be transferred – conduction, convection and radiation.

Read the text on the left to remind you how heat is transferred.

Conduction

This is when a substance transfers energy, without the substance itself moving. For example, if one part of a metal bar is hot and the other part cool, then heat is transferred to the cooler part – the metal does not move.

Metals are good **conductors** of heat. Non-metals (such as wood) are generally poor conductors. They are called **insulators**.

Gases are very poor conductors. For example, a fluffy duvet contains more air than a thin duvet, so less heat moves from your body to the chilly bedroom.

Convection

Liquids and gases can flow, and so they can move heat energy from a hotter place to a colder place. This is called **convection**. A good example is a heater in a room.

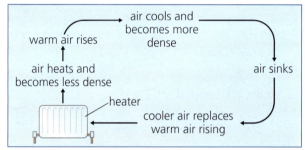

Convection

Radiation

Energy is being transferred to and from all objects, all the time, by **radiation**. This can happen through empty space (a vacuum). For example, if you go outside and stand in the sunshine your body warms up. The Sun's energy has been radiated through space.

Conduction
only through solids.
Convection
by liquids and gases.
Radiation
can pass through space.

More about radiation

Hot bodies, like the Sun, give off infra red radiation. The hotter the body, the more radiation is given off (emitted).

Dark, dull surfaces emit a lot of radiation. They also absorb a lot of radiation. Shiny, white surfaces are poor emitters of radiation and do not absorb much either.

This is why houses and cars in hot countries are often painted white, to keep the insides cool.

Radiation from the Sun

Using insulation

The ideas of heat loss and insulation can be used to prevent heat loss from a house.

Most ways of insulating a house are based on the fact that air is a very poor conductor of heat. They include:

- double glazing – traps a layer of air between two panes of glass

- fibreglass lagging in the roof – traps air within the layers of fibreglass

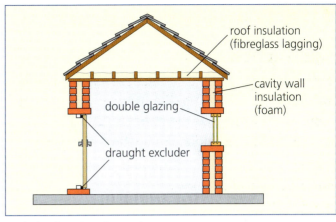

Reducing heat loss from a house

- cavity walls – the gaps between the bricks are filled with air

- cavity wall insulation – foam in the cavity traps air, so it cannot rise (by convection) even when it warms up.

- draught excluder – strips of foam around a door frame make a tight-fitting door, so warm air cannot escape.

The different ways of reducing heat loss from a house cost different amounts of money. Some are better value than others. For example, draught excluders cost very little but save a lot of heat. On the other hand, double glazing costs a lot of money compared to the amount of energy it saves.

In an examination you may be given figures to work out how effective the different methods are. This is likely to include actual figures for cost and how much you save per year in reduced fuel bills. You can then work out how long it takes to 'get your money back' from what you pay out in the first place.

Worked example

Q Mrs Brown paid £3000 to have her house double-glazed. Her central heating bill over the following year went down from £480 to £440.
How many years will it take for Mrs Brown to have saved enough on her heating bills to cover the cost of the double glazing?

A Amount saved per year
= £480 − £440 = £40

$$\frac{£3000}{£40} = 75 \text{ years}$$

Questions

1 Copy and complete the sentences using these words:

   conduction insulation radiation convection

   The transfer of heat through a solid is known as _____ . If the transfer of the heat can take place through space this is known as _____ .
   A material that prevents heat loss is a form of _____ . The movement of gas or a liquid in heat loss is known as _____ .

2 Why are most cars in Spain white in colour?

3 Why does fibreglass lagging prevent heat loss through the roof of a house?

Electrical energy

Electrical energy is easily transferred as heat, light, sound and movement energy. This makes it very useful in the home and in industry.

Many household appliances use electricity:

- heaters (for example, fan heaters, electric bar heaters)
- light (for example, light bulbs, television)
- sound (for example, radio, television, stereo systems)
- movement (for example, food processors, hair driers).

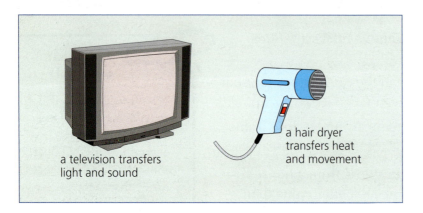

a television transfers light and sound

a hair dryer transfers heat and movement

Measuring energy

We measure energy in joules (J).

How much electrical energy an appliance transfers depends on:

- how long the appliance is switched on
- how fast the appliance transfers energy (its **power**).

1 kW = 1000 W.
1 watt is the transfer of 1 joule of energy in 1 second.

We measure power in watts (W) or kilowatts (kW). The greater the power, the more energy is transferred in a given time – as shown by the formula:

$$\text{power (watt/W)} = \frac{\text{energy transferred (joule/J)}}{\text{time taken (second/s)}}$$

1 watt is the transfer of 1 joule of energy in 1 second. You can rearrange the formula to find out the amount of electrical energy transferred (used) by an appliance:

$$\text{energy transferred (joule/J)} = \text{power (watt/W)} \times \text{time (second/s)}$$

How much does the electricity used cost?

This depends on how much the appliance uses (transfers). It will cost more the longer the appliance is switched on and the faster it transfers electricity (its power).

The energy transferred from the mains is measured in kilowatt hours (kWh), which are also called **units**. Electricity bills are costed in units.

Units are worked out using the same formula as before but using kW per hour not W per second:

> **energy transferred** = **power** × **time**
> (kilowatt hour/kWh)   (kilowatt/kW)   (hour/h)

To calculate the cost of the electricity use this formula:

> **total cost = number of units × cost per unit**

For example, if you have used 434 units at 42p for each unit the cost will be:

434 units × 42p = £182.28

How efficient are appliances?

In all appliances some of the energy is used usefully – and some is wasted. For example: an electric mixer – the useful energy is movement, and the wasted energy is noise and heat (it will warm up).

The wasted energy is usually lost. It is very difficult to 'capture' this wasted energy because it spreads out quickly – it cannot be used again.

An appliance is said to be **efficient** when it usefully transfers most of the energy supplied to it. Efficiency can be measured using this formula:

> **efficiency** = $\dfrac{\text{useful energy transferred by device}}{\text{total energy supplied to device}}$

Questions

1 Draw a spider diagram to show at least **three** household appliances that transfer electricity to **useful** sound energy. Put **sound** at the centre of your diagram.

2 A microwave transfers 6000 J of energy in 8 s. What is its power rating?

A 100 W light bulb is brighter than a 60 W light bulb because it is transferring (using) more electricity in the same time.

Worked example

Q A fan heater has a rating of 2 kW. It is switched on for 90 minutes.

How much energy is transferred?

A energy transferred
= power × time
= 2 × 1.5
(90 minutes is 1.5 hours)
= 3 kilowatt hours

Worked example

Q A fan heater transfers 20 000 J of useful energy when switched on. However, in the same period of time 80 000 J of energy are transferred to the fan heater. What is the efficiency of the fan heater?

A
Efficiency
= $\dfrac{\text{useful energy transferred}}{\text{total energy transferred}}$
= $\dfrac{20\,000}{80\,000}$
= 0.25
= 25%

Generating electricity

Mains electricity is produced in power stations. In most power stations, fossil fuels are burned to heat water. Other power stations use nuclear fuels (for example, uranium and plutonium). The steam that is produced is used to drive **turbines**, which drive **generators** to make electricity.

Fossil fuels

When fossil fuels are burned carbon dioxide is released into the atmosphere. This increases the Greenhouse Effect, which results in increased global warming.

If you compare the amounts of fossils fuels needed to produce the same amount of energy, coal releases more carbon dioxide than oil, and oil releases more carbon dioxide than natural gas. In other words, coal is the most polluting of the fossil fuels.

Most coal and oil also release sulphur dioxide, which then causes acid rain. The sulphur can be removed from the fuel or the sulphur dioxide from the waste gas. This increases the cost of the energy produced.

Nuclear fuels

Unlike fossil fuels, nuclear fuels do not produce polluting waste gases. When running normally, very little radiation escapes into the surroundings. But although they are 'clean' fuels, if something does go wrong (such as an accident) the effects are very serious. Large amounts of dangerously radioactive material can escape and be carried great distances. Also, the waste material nuclear power stations produce may stay dangerously radioactive for thousands of years. It has to be stored very safely.

Fossils fuels (coal, oil and gas) are non-renewable sources of energy. It would take millions of years to replace the amounts we have used. It is important not to use more than we really need, and to find other sources of energy. Renewable energy sources include wood (because trees can be grown to replace those cut down), sunlight, the wind, the waves, running water and the tides. These energy sources will not run out.

For more about the Greenhouse Effect and acid rain, see the section on *Environment* pages 30–31.

Renewable energy sources

Electricity can also be generated from renewable energy sources. Some drive turbines directly. For example:

- the wind
- the rise and fall of water due to waves
- the flow of water from a higher level to a lower level from behind tidal barrages or the dams of hydroelectric schemes.

Other renewable sources include geothermal energy (heat produced below the Earth) and the Sun's radiation.
All these forms of renewable energy have their advantages and disadvantages, including the different effects they have on the environment.

Wind farms

Wind turbines are a 'clean' source of energy because they produce no chemical pollution. However, you need many wind turbines to produce a reasonable amount of electricity. They have to be built where there is plenty of wind (for example, on hilltops), which can be an eyesore and a source of noise pollution for people living nearby. It is difficult to control the supply of electricity because this depends on the amount of wind.

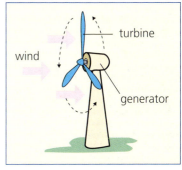

Wind power

Tidal power

The rise and fall of sea level with the tides can be used to turn turbines and generate electricity. The supply of electricity is reliable because tides are regular and sea levels predictable. There is no chemical pollution, but barrages of turbines placed across estuaries can obstruct shipping and destroy wildlife habitats. For example, estuaries are home to wading birds that feed on mud-living organisms. The mud-living organisms, and therefore the birds, will disappear from the area if barrages are built there.

Tidal power

Hydroelectricity

These power stations can only be built where there is a ready supply of running water (for example, mountain areas of Scotland). There is no chemical pollution, but reservoirs need to be made (often by damming rivers) to store water. This means flooding land that may have been used for farming and forestry, and destroying wildlife habitats. Electricity can be produced quickly and reliably by releasing water from the reservoir.

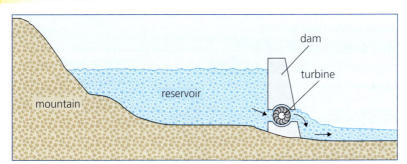

Hydroelectric power

Generating electricity continued

Solar cells ●

Solar cells use light energy from the Sun to produce electricity, but at a high cost. The electricity produced costs more than any other except for that stored in non-rechargeable batteries. Even so, they are often the best choice in very remote locations (for example, on satellites in space) and when you only need very small amounts of electricity (for example, watches and calculators).

Geothermal energy

In some volcanic regions, hot water and steam rise to the surface. This can be used to turn turbines and generate electricity. The heat comes from underground rocks containing radioactive elements, such as uranium. As these elements slowly decay, they produce geothermal energy. They are sometimes described as

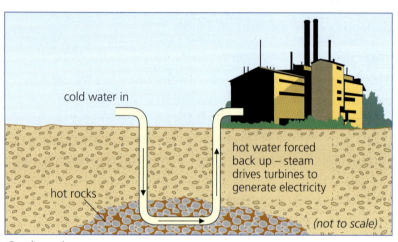

Geothermal power

'hot rocks'. Building geothermal power stations can be expensive, but this is a reliable energy source because the hot rocks are always there and always hot.

The best energy source?

So what is the best way of generating electricity?

This depends on a number of different things. All the energy sources described have their advantages and disadvantages. The cleanest source might be the least reliable or too expensive to be cost-effective, or the easiest to obtain may be the most polluting.

Power stations are reliable as they produce electricity at any time of day or night. However, the time it takes to start-up a power station varies a lot.

Fuel	Time to start-up power station
nuclear	longest time
coal	↑
oil	
natural gas·	shortest time

Some renewable sources are less reliable:

- Wind generators depend on whether the wind is blowing.

- Tidal barrages depend on whether the tide is going in or out. How high the tide is also varies from day to day and month to month throughout the year.

- Solar cells work only when sufficient light falls on them. If the sun is shining brightly they will produce a lot but on a dull day not very much. At night they produce nothing!

Other renewable energy sources are more reliable and more energy-efficient. For example, hydroelectric stations can be started quickly by allowing the water to flow. When there is excess electricity available from other sources water can even be pumped back to the top lake or reservoir. This uses electricity that would have been wasted.

It is worth taking time to understand the advantages and disadvantages of the different ways of generating electricity. In an examination you may be asked to discuss them.

Questions

1. Draw a table with the headings **Non-renewable** and **Renewable**. Write at least **three** examples of energy sources in each column.

2. Suggest **two** advantages and **two** disadvantages of wind farms as a source of energy.

3. Suggest **two** reasons why nuclear power is so expensive.

4. Hydroelectric power is relatively cheap and renewable. What is the major disadvantage of hydroelectric power?

Module test questions

1 This question is about energy transfer.

Match words from the list with the numbers 1–4 in the table.

radiation
insulation
conduction
convection

	Description
1	heat transfer through the movement of a gas
2	prevention of heat loss
3	heat transfer through a solid
4	heat transfer by waves

2 Match the symbols in the list with the spaces 1–4 to complete these sentences.

kWh J W s

The unit of power is ____**1**____ .
The unit of energy is ____**2**____ .
The unit of time is ____**3**____ .
The unit for the cost of electricity is ____**4**____ .

3 This question is about how household appliances transfer electrical energy.

Match the appliances in the list to the numbers 1–4 in the table.

radio
toaster
torch
food mixer

	Description of energy transfer
1	electrical to movement
2	electrical to sound
3	electrical to heat
4	electrical to light

4 The table below describes different energy sources.

Match each of the sources in the list with the best description 1–4 in the table.

coal
uranium
solar
hydroelectric

	Description
1	the source for nuclear energy
2	burned to heat water
3	running water drives the turbines
4	converts energy directly from the Sun

5 Which **two** types of energy transfer best describe useful energy transfer by a television?

A movement
B heat
C light
D sound
E chemical.

6 Which **two** methods of electricity generation represent non-renewable energy sources?

A wind
B coal
C hydroelectric
D solar
E nuclear.

7 The diagram shows various forms of house insulation.

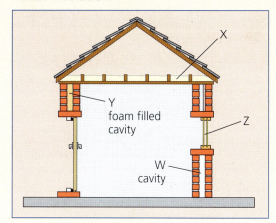

1. The insulation at X:

   A prevents radiation of heat
   B traps air and prevents convection
   C is made of fibreglass, which prevents conduction
   D is expensive and saves little money.

2. The insulation at Y is more effective than W because the foam:

   A conducts heat through the wall
   B prevents radiation of heat
   C replaces air, which is a good conductor
   D prevents air rising, so reducing heat loss by convection.

3. The insulation at Z:

   A is cheap and not effective
   B is expensive and effective
   C is expensive and not effective
   D is cheap and effective.

4. Another good way of insulating the house would be to:

   A replace thin curtains with thick ones
   B leave doors open to let air circulate
   C keep the house very warm
   D control the temperature of all the radiators.

8 This is a hair drier.

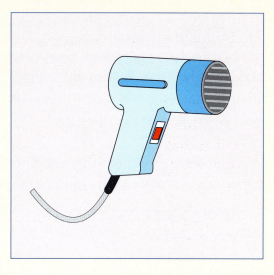

1. In which **two** of the following ways is energy usefully transferred?

   A heat and sound
   B light and heat
   C heat and movement
   D movement and sound.

2. One watt is the transfer of:

   A one joule of energy in one minute
   B one joule of energy in one second
   C 1000 J of energy in one second
   D 1000 J of energy in one minute.

3. This hair drier transfers 1000 J in 20 s. What is its power rating? Use this equation:

   $$\text{power} = \frac{\text{energy transferred}}{\text{time}}$$

   A 0.2 W
   B 50 W
   C 0.5 W
   D 200 W

4. An electricity bill is costed on the number of units you have used. What is one unit?

   A a watt hour
   B a watt minute
   C a kilowatt hour
   D a kilowatt minute.

Electrical circuits

Electrical current flows through **circuits**. Current is a flow of electrons (**charge**). It transfers energy to **components** such as light bulbs, heaters and motors (for example, in washing machines, hair driers, lawnmowers). Electrical current is measured in amperes (amps).

A circuit has a source of electrical power (for example, a battery or mains electricity) and components.

Components resist the flow of electricity. **Resistance** is a measure of how easy or difficult it is for the current to flow.

Voltage

The electric current is 'pushed' around a circuit by the **voltage** of the power supply. (Voltage is also called **potential difference** or **p.d.**) A small battery is about 1.5 volts. A car battery is 12 volts. Mains electricity is 230 volts.

Potential difference is the difference in energy between two points in an electrical circuit. It is also called voltage.

A battery is made up of **cells** connected in **series**. If you connect up two or more cells in series, the voltage they provide for a circuit is the sum (total) of all their voltages.

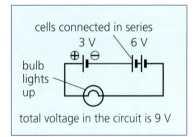

Cells connected in series

Circuits in series

If the components of a circuit are connected in series:

■ the same amount of current flows through each component (the current has no alternative but to flow through all the components)

■ the voltage (potential difference) of the electricity supply is shared between the components

■ the resistance of the circuit is the resistance of each component added together.

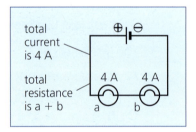

A circuit in series

Circuits in parallel

If the components are connected in **parallel**:

■ the full voltage (p.d.) of the circuit goes through each component, but

■ the current in the circuit 'splits' to travel through different components (current can flow most easily through the component with the smallest resistance)

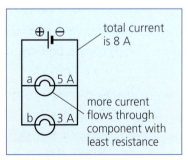

A circuit in parallel

- the total current in the whole circuit is the sum of the currents through the separate components
- the total resistance is the sum of the resistance of each component.

Circuit symbols ●

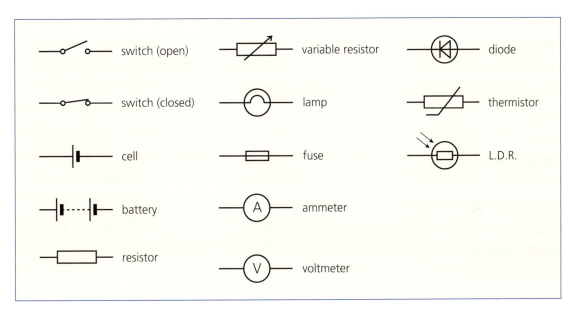

switch (open) variable resistor diode

switch (closed) lamp thermistor

cell fuse L.D.R.

battery ammeter

resistor voltmeter

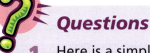

Questions

1 Here is a simple electrical circuit connected in series.

a What is the component X?

b What is the component Y?

c What is the total current flowing?

d If each cell is 3 V, what is the total p.d. (potential difference) of the circuit?

e How much p.d. is there across each component?

2 Copy and complete these sentences, using words from this list:

adding   components   cell   subtracting

The current for the circuit is provided by a _____ . The total current in the circuit is _____ the current flowing through the different _____ .

3 a What happens to the current in a circuit if it passes through **two** components in parallel?

b How is this different to what happens if the current passes through components in series?

Power, voltage and resistance

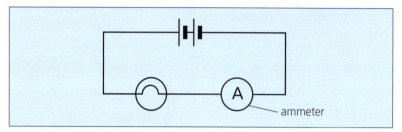

An ammeter is connected in series

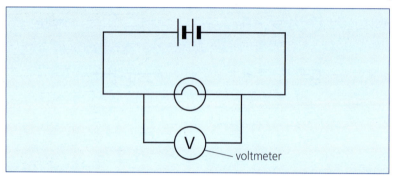

A voltmeter is connected across the component

You can measure the current (in amps) flowing through a component by using an **ammeter**.

You can measure voltage (potential difference) flowing across a component by using a **voltmeter**.

Working out power

Once you know the current and voltage flowing through and across a component, you can work out how much energy is being transferred to the appliance. Multiply voltage by current and you have the amount of energy being transferred every second. This measurement is the **power rating** and is given in watts.

The rate of energy transfer is shown by this formula.

| **power** (watt/W) | = | **potential difference** (volt/V) | × | **current** (ampere/A) |

All appliances have a power rating. For example, light bulbs can be 100 W, 60 W or 40 W.

Resistance

Resistance is a measure of how difficult it is for a current to flow. It is measured in ohms (Ω). All electrical appliances or components in a circuit resist the current. The bigger the resistance, the less current flows through the appliance. In other words, you need a bigger voltage (push) to get the same amount of current through the component.

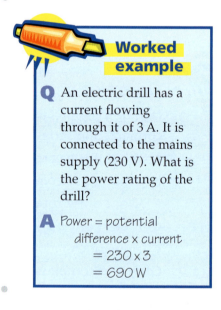

Worked example

Q An electric drill has a current flowing through it of 3 A. It is connected to the mains supply (230 V). What is the power rating of the drill?

A Power = potential difference × current
   = 230 × 3
   = 690 W

Current-voltage graphs show how current through a component varies with the voltage across it. The graphs on the right show what happens in three electrical components.

■ A *resistor* is a component that reduces the current passing through a circuit. As the voltage increases across a resistor, the current also increases at the same rate. In other words, the current is proportional to the voltage across a resistor (at a constant temperature).

■ In a *filament* (such as in a light bulb), as the voltage increases, so does the current. But at higher values (that is, when the filament gets hotter) the resistance of the filament is greater. This means that the increase in the current flowing through the filament is smaller at higher temperatures.

■ A *diode* is a component that allows current to flow in only one direction. When the voltage is reversed, almost no current flows – because the resistance of the diode is very high in the reverse direction.

You need to know two other facts about resistance:

■ The resistance of a *light-dependent resistor* decreases as the light intensity increases. This type of resistor allows more current through it as the amount of light increases.

■ The resistance of a *thermistor* (a 'thermal resistor') decreases as the temperature increases. This type of resistor allows more current to flow when it is hotter.

Working out potential difference

The relationship between resistance, current and potential difference is shown by this formula:

potential difference = current × resistance
(volt/V)   (ampere/A)   (ohm/Ω)

Given the current flowing through a circuit and the resistance of the components in the circuit, you can work out the potential difference.

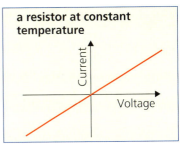

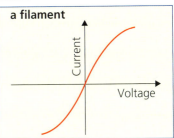

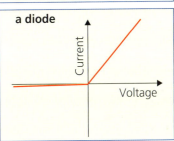

Current–voltage graphs

Worked example

Q A circuit has a current flowing through it of 8 A and has a resistance of 3 Ω. What is the potential difference being provided to the circuit?

A potential difference
= current × resistance
= 8 × 3
= 24 V

Questions

1 An electric saw is plugged into the mains (230 V). A current of 5 A flows through it. What is the power rating of the saw?

2 Copy and complete the sentences using these words: **amperes   watts   volts**

Potential difference is measured in _____ . Power is measured in _____ .

Current is measured in _____ .

Static electricity and electrical charge

Static electricity

In solid conductors (for example, copper wires) the electric current is a flow of electrons.

Many materials are not good conductors – electrons will not flow freely through them. These materials can build up an electrical charge. If you take two materials and rub them together (for example, a plastic strip and a dry woollen cloth), electrons will pass from one to the other. The material losing electrons becomes positively charged (+). The material gaining electrons becomes negatively charged (−). This is **static electricity** and the materials are **electrically charged**.

A charged object can attract small, light objects. So, for example, if you charge up a balloon against your jumper and then hold it against your hair it will often attract your hair.

Two objects with the same charge repel each other. Two objects with opposite charges attract each other.

two different plastic strips rubbed with a dry woollen cloth

they will attract

Static electricity

Making use of static electricity

This is what happens in a **photocopier**:

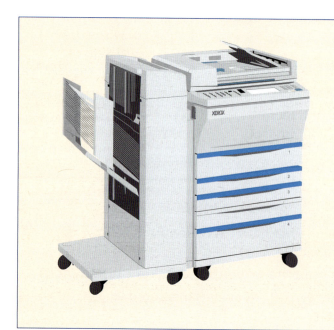

1. A copying plate is electronically charged.
2. The image of what you want to copy is projected on to the plate.
3. Where light from the copier bulb falls on the plate, the charges leak away.
4. The parts of the plate that still have a charge attract the black powder.
5. This powder is transferred from the plate to a sheet of photocopy paper.
6. The paper is heated and the powder sticks.
7. You now have your photocopy!

This is what happens in an **electrostatic smoke precipitator**:

Burning fossil fuels in power stations pollutes the atmosphere. Smoke is part of the pollution produced. Smoke is tiny particles of solid matter. It is removed by using the principles of electrostatics using a smoke precipitator.

1 On the way up the chimney the smoke in the waste gases passes through a negatively charged grid.

3 The smoke particles become negatively charged and are therefore repelled by the grid.

3 They are attracted by the positively charged collecting plates lining the chimney walls.

4 These positively charged metal plates are attached to Earth.

5 The smoke particles now lose their charge and drop to the bottom where they are collected.

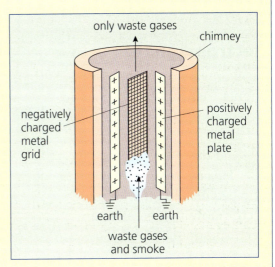

Electrolysis

If ionic compounds (for example, common salt, NaCl) are melted or dissolved in water they conduct electricity. The current is caused by negatively charged ions (for example, Cl^-) moving to the positive electrode, and positively charged ions (for example, Na^+) moving to the negative electrode. Some of the elements in compounds are released at the electrodes. This is called **electrolysis**.

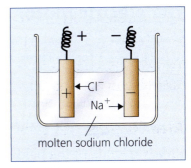

Electrolysis

Questions

1 Copy and complete these sentences about static electricity. Use words from this list:

negatively rub positively charge

If you _____ two materials together then you may build up a _____. Electrons may pass from one material to another. The material losing electrons will become _____ charged, and the material gaining electrons will become _____ charged.

2 Why do some parts of the photocopying plate on a photocopier attract the black powder and some do not?

3 Why do substances have to be dissolved or molten before electrolysis can take place?

Making things move

Electric currents produce magnetic fields. These can be used to make things move.

Electromagnets

A coil of wire can behave like a magnet – when it has an electric current running through it. One end of the coil becomes a north pole and the other end a south pole. This is a magnet that can be switched on and off with the electric current. It is called an **electromagnet**.

If you reverse the current, you reverse the poles of the magnet.

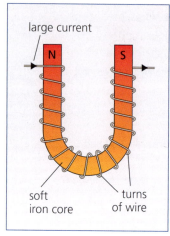

large current

N S

soft iron core   turns of wire

A simple electromagnet

A **bar magnet** has a north pole and a south pole. Opposite poles attract. Similar poles repel.

It also has a **magnetic field** around it, which has an effect on any nearby magnetic material (for example, iron or steel or another magnet).

The electric motor

If you place a wire carrying a current in a magnetic field, it experiences a force. The size of this force can be increased by:

- increasing the strength of the magnetic field
- increasing the size of the current flowing through the wire.

If the direction of the field or the current is reversed, the wire experiences an opposite force.

This is basically how an electric d.c. (direct current) motor works – a coil of wire turns or spins because of magnetic forces.

The difference between direct current (d.c.) and alternating current (a.c.) is explained on page 107.

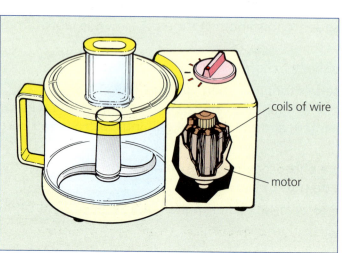

coils of wire

motor

The door bell

The electromagnet in this case is used to work a bell push.

This is how it works.

1. You press the bell push. The circuit is complete and a current flows.

2. The electromagnet works and pulls the soft iron. The hammer hits the gong.

3. The contact screw is not now contacting the springy metal strip. The circuit therefore breaks and the electromagnet stops working.

4. The hammer springs back. The contact screw is now in contact again with the springy metal strip, so the circuit is complete again and the current flows.

5. The bell continues to ring (the hammer keeps hitting the gong) until you take your finger off the bell push and break the circuit.

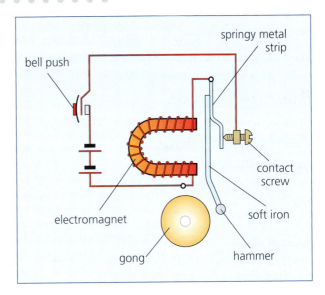

When you press the bell push, the circuit is continually broken and remade. So the hammer doesn't just hit the gong once, but continues to hit it until you release the bell push.

The loudspeaker

The electromagnet is used to create sound waves.

This is how it works.

1. As a current flows through the coil it develops a magnetic force.

2. The magnet also has a field and the magnet and the coil interact.

3. The cone moves (vibrates) in and out.

4. These vibrations result in sound waves.

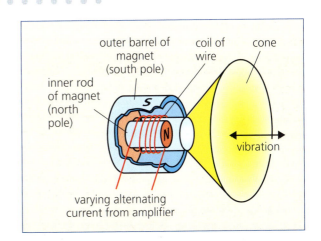

Questions

1. What happens to the poles of the electromagnet if the current is reversed?

2. Give **two** ways of increasing the force produced by an electric motor.

Mains electricity

Our electricity supply is about 230 V. This can kill if it is not used safely. Most appliances are connected to the mains by a cable and a three-pin plug. Wiring plugs correctly and using the correct fuses are two important parts of electrical safety.

Cables and plugs

The cable has:

- two or three inner wires of copper (a good conductor) to carry the current
- an outer, flexible cover made of plastic (a good insulator) to prevent the current flowing through anyone handling the cable.

The plug has:

- a plastic or rubber case (a good insulator)
- pins (to fit in the socket) made of brass (a good conductor)
- a fuse
- an earth pin
- a cable grip.

How to connect the plug

The correct way to do this is:

- blue wire connected to neutral terminal
- brown wire connected through the fuse to the live terminal
- green/yellow wire (if fitted) connected to earth terminal
- cable grip to hold the cable securely in place for safety
- the correct rating of fuse.

You must be able to identify errors in the wiring of a plug.

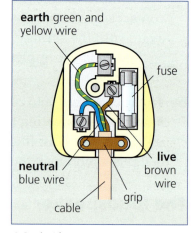

A 3-pin plug

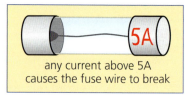

A 5 amp fuse

Safety devices

Fuses

The fuse has a current rating. That is, a certain level of current can flow through it. A 13 amp fuse will take a current of 13 amps. If a higher current flows through the fuse, it melts or breaks. This breaks the circuit and stops the current going through the appliance. A current that is too high could damage the appliance and also cause a fire.

Appliances have a fuse rating a little higher than their own current rating otherwise the circuit would keep breaking. You should always use the recommended fuse rating.

Earth

If an appliance has a metal case (such as a toaster) it should be **earthed**. This is a safety measure to prevent you getting an electric shock if, by fault, the metal case is connected to the live wire. The large current would flow to the 'earth' connection in the plug, and the fuse would break. To earth an appliance you connect the earth pin to the metal case through the yellow/green wire.

Circuit breakers

Circuit breakers are increasingly used instead of fuses in some appliances. They contain an electromagnet. When the current becomes high enough, then the strength of the electromagnet increases enough to separate a pair of contacts. This breaks the circuit. Circuit breakers work more quickly than fuses and are easy to reset by pressing a button.

a.c./d.c.

Mains electricity supplied to your home has an **alternating current** (it is described as a.c.). This means that it is constantly changing direction. In the UK it has a frequency of 50 cycles per second or 50 Hertz (Hz). This means the current changes direction and back again 50 times each second.

Cells and batteries are different. They supply a current that is always flowing in the same direction. This is called **direct current** (d.c.).

You can see the difference between a.c. and d.c. in these diagrams. They show the patterns you would see on an **oscilloscope**.

Electric motors that work from mains electricity are designed to convert a.c. into d.c. They use a split ring to keep switching the direction of the current, so that it always moves in one direction. You do not need to know how a split ring works.

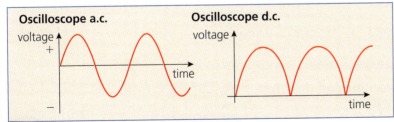

Oscilloscope a.c.

Oscilloscope d.c.

Questions

1. This question is about wiring up a plug. Copy and complete the table using these words:

   blue   brown   green/yellow

	Colour of wire
neutral	
earth	
live	

2. Suggest **two** ways in which circuit breakers are better than fuses.

Making and supplying electricity

The generator

If you rotate a coil of wire in a magnetic field then you will induce an electric current. This is how the **generator** works.

Other ways of generating electricity would be to rotate the magnets around the coil, or to move a magnet in and out of a coil.

The current is reversed:

- when you move the magnet into, then out of, the coil
- if you move the other pole of the magnet into the coil.

As the coil of wire cuts through the lines of force of the magnetic field, a voltage (potential difference) is produced between the ends of the wire. If the wire is part of a complete circuit then a current will flow. This is how a bicycle dynamo lamp works.

> **The generator** – spinning movement within magnetic field = electrical current.
> **The motor** – electrical current within magnetic field = spinning movement.

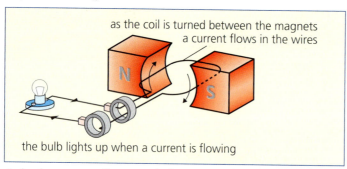

as the coil is turned between the magnets a current flows in the wires

the bulb lights up when a current is flowing

A simple generator (for example, bicycle dynamo)

You can increase the size of the voltage by doing any, or all, of the following things:

- move the wire faster
- increase the strength of the magnetic field
- increase the number of turns on the coil of wire
- increase the area of the coil.

This is the principle behind electricity generating power stations. In most power stations steam is used to drive turbines, which in turn drive the generators. The generators then produce electricity.

Using tidal or hydroelectric power, it is water that drives the turbines. Steam does not need to be produced by burning fossil fuels so these methods are environmentally more 'friendly'.

Transformers

These are used to change the voltage in an a.c. supply. Power lines carry electricity through the National Grid at 250 000 volts – not much use for your television! Transformers bring it back down to 230 volts.

As the electricity leaves the power station, transformers increase the voltage to transmit it efficiently through the power lines. Transformers near homes then reduce this voltage so that it can be used with household appliances.

The higher the voltage transmitted in our power lines, the smaller the current needed to transmit electricity at the same rate. A high current would heat up the power lines and so waste energy.

Mains current is a.c. because:
- it is easier to produce
- only a.c. can be transformed (stepped up or down) for transmission.

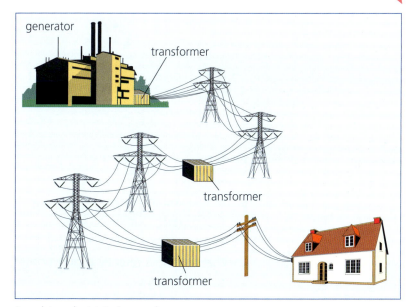

Supplying electricity to your home

Questions

1. Draw a spider diagram to show **three** different ways of increasing the voltage produced by a generator. Put **increasing voltage** at the centre of your diagram.

2. Copy and complete the sentences using these words:

   potential difference   rotated   magnetic field   lines of force

   To produce electricity a coil of wire is _____ in a _____ . The wire cuts through the _____ . A voltage (_____) is produced between the ends of the wire.

3. Why do we use transformers?

Module test questions

1 The diagram shows some components that may be found as part of an electrical circuit.

Choose words from the list for each of the components 1–4 in the diagram.

resistor
diode
fuse
thermistor

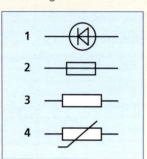

2 This question is about using a plug safely.

Copy and complete the table using words from this list.

fuse
blue wire
brown wire
green/yellow wire

	Inside a plug
1	connected to the earth
2	connected to the neutral
3	protects the circuit
4	connected to the live

3 This question is about how a loudspeaker works.

Sentences 1–4 describe what happens when you use a loudspeaker. Put the sentences into the correct order.

1 the cone vibrates in and out
2 the current flows and the coil develops a magnetic field
3 the vibrations produce sound
4 the field of the coil interacts with the magnets.

4 Match the units in this list with each of numbers 1–4 in the table.

hertz   volt   ampere   watt

	What does the unit represent?
1	power
2	frequency
3	current
4	potential difference

5 Which **two** of these statements are true of the graph showing current against volts?

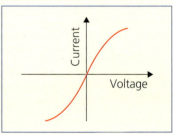

A there is no current if the voltage is reversed
B as the voltage increases so does the current, but eventually the current increases more slowly
C the current is directly proportional to the voltage
D when the voltage is reversed the current still increases as the voltage increases
E the current is inversely proportional to the voltage.

6 This is a diagram of a circuit with two light bulbs set up in parallel.

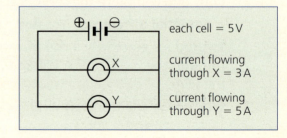

each cell = 5 V

current flowing through X = 3 A

current flowing through Y = 5 A

Which **two** of these statements about the circuit are correct?

    A the total potential difference produced by the cells is 5 V

    B the total current in the circuit is 5 A

    C the resistance in the circuit is equal to that of the more resistant bulb

    D the total current in the circuit is 8 A

    E the total potential difference in the circuit is 10 V.

7 This is a diagram of a bell push circuit. It uses an electromagnet.

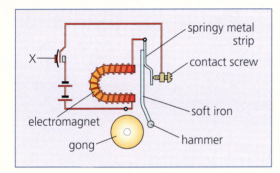

1. What happens when you press X?

    A the circuit breaks

    B the electromagnet stops working

    C a current flows

    D the soft iron springs back from the electromagnet.

2. What happens as the hammer hits the gong?

    A the circuit is completed

    B the electromagnet starts to work

    C the current stops flowing

    D the contact screws start to touch the springy metal strip.

3. What happens when the circuit is broken?

    A the current stops flowing

    B the hammer hits the gong

    C the electromagnet continues to work

    D the soft iron is attracted to the electromagnet.

4. How could you increase the strength of the electromagnet?

    A decreasing the current

    B using thicker wires in the coil

    C making the electromagnet thinner

    D using more turns of wire for the coil.

8 This is a diagram of a generator.

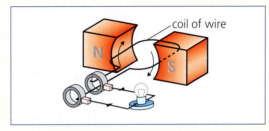

1. When the coil spins:

    A a voltage is induced

    B the resistance of the coil increases

    C the bulb goes out

    D the coil sets up its own magnetic field.

2. Which of the following would not increase the voltage?

    A increasing the strength of the magnetic field

    B decreasing the area of the coil

    C moving the wire faster

    D increasing the number of turns on the coil.

3. In which of the following forms of power generation is water not turned into steam?

    A coal fired   **B** nuclear

    C gas fired   **D** hydroelectric.

4. Transformers are used at power stations to:

    A decrease the resistance of power lines

    B alter the voltage

    C allow a greater current to flow

    D increase the temperature at which the wires transmit the electricity.

Speed, velocity and acceleration

Speed

You have already learned how to work out the speed of an object travelling in a straight line. You use this formula:

$$\text{speed (m/s)} = \frac{\text{distance travelled (m)}}{\text{time (s)}}$$

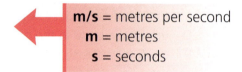

m/s = metres per second
m = metres
s = seconds

You can also show this on a distance-time graph.

You can see in this graph that as time passes the object does not go any further. It is standing still.

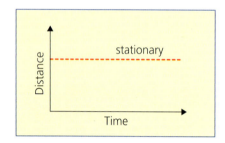

You can see in this graph that as time passes the object is moving further away. The line is straight, which means the object is moving at a steady speed.

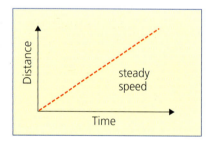

The steeper the slope of the graph, the faster the object is travelling.

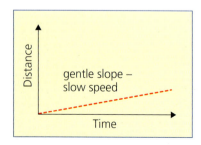

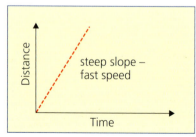

The steeper the slope of the graph, the further the object will travel in the same time.

Velocity

Velocity is speed in a straight line.

If you go for a bike ride you will take many left and right turns. You can work out your speed at the end by how far you have ridden in how much time. You would have to ride your bike in a straight line to be able to work out your velocity.

Velocity–time graphs show how an object moves.

Graph **A** shows constant velocity. The object is not getting any faster or slower over time. It is going at the same velocity.

Graph **B** shows that the object is getting faster as time passes. It is **accelerating**. The graph is a straight line, which means the acceleration is constant.

The acceleration of an object is the rate at which its velocity changes. You can work out an object's acceleration using this formula:

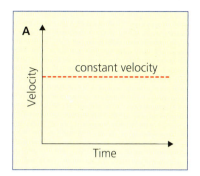

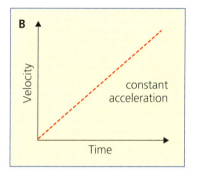

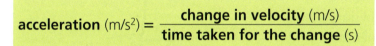

$$\text{acceleration (m/s}^2) = \frac{\text{change in velocity (m/s)}}{\text{time taken for the change (s)}}$$

Worked example

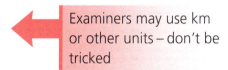

Examiners may use km or other units – don't be tricked

Q A car accelerates from 0 to 30 m/s in 10 seconds. What is the acceleration of the car?

A $\text{acceleration} = \frac{\text{change in velocity}}{\text{time}}$

$= \frac{30}{10} = 3 \text{ m/s}^2$

(always remember the units)

Questions

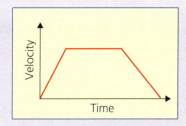

1 A car travels 5000 metres in 200 seconds. What is its speed?

2 An aeroplane accelerates along the runway. In 8 seconds it accelerates from 0 to 56 m/s. What is its acceleration?

3 This graph shows the movement of a car. Study the graph then describe what is happening to the car.

Speeding up and slowing down

Everything is affected by the forces around it. The force from your hand moves the pen and you write. The force of your arm acts on your coffee mug to raise it to your mouth.

Balanced forces

If the forces on an object cancel each other out, there is no change in the object. If it is sitting still, it stays sitting still.

The forces are **balanced**, so they have no overall effect. If the forces on a moving object are balanced, it carries on at the same speed and in the same direction.

For example:

- if a car is not moving and you don't change the forces acting on it, the car will remain not moving
- if the car is already moving and you don't change the forces acting on it, then the car keeps moving at the same speed.

When an object rests on a surface:
- the weight of the object causes a downward force
- the surface exerts an upwards force.

The two forces are the same – they are **balanced**.

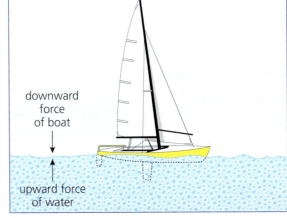

downward force of boat

upward force of water

Balanced forces

What happens if you change the forces?

If the forces change, the movement of the object changes.

When a car engine starts, it gives a stationary car greater forward force so the car moves forward.

When the car is moving forward, a greater forward force makes it move forward faster.

When the car is moving forward, a greater opposite force makes it slow down.

In these diagrams, the size of the arrows shows the size of the forces

car moves forward

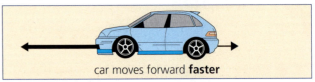

car moves forward **faster**

car moving forward **now slows down**

When the car is moving forward, the greater the forward force the faster it will go.

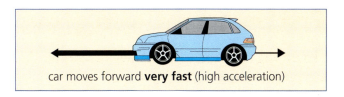

car moves forward **very fast** (high acceleration)

Forces that are not equal are said to be **unbalanced**.

You may have heard the expression '0 to 60 in so-many seconds'. This is a way car manufacturers describe how quickly their cars can accelerate. The heavier the car, the more force it takes to give the car a particular acceleration. Or to look at it another way – the more powerful the engine, the more force it exerts on the car, so the faster the car will accelerate.

Just think how fast a lightweight car with a big engine will accelerate!

The force of gravity

Objects fall to Earth because of **gravity**. Gravity is a downward force. On Earth the acceleration due to gravity is about 10 N/kg. Your weight is actually your mass in kilograms multiplied by the force of gravity:

Weight is often wrongly given in kilograms – bathroom scales show kilograms. This is actually your mass. Your weight is measured in newtons.

weight (N) = mass (kg) × force of gravity (N/kg)

Worked example

Q You have a friend whose mass is 45 kg. What is her weight?

A weight = mass × force of gravity
= 45 × 10
= 450 N (remember the units)

Cover the page, then write down the units for:
weight
mass
the force of gravity.
Check your answer.

Questions

1 A car takes 5 seconds to reach a speed of 30 m/s from standing still. What is its acceleration?

2 Find out your mass in kilograms. What is your weight in newtons?

3 Describe the size of the forces when:
   a a car is speeding up
   b a car is slowing down.

Friction

Friction always acts in the opposite direction to the way the object is moving.

For example:

- if you are swimming, the force of friction slows you down through the water
- when an aeroplane flies through the air, the force of friction (air resistance) is acting to slow it down.

The force of friction acts:
- when an object moves through air or water
- when solid surfaces slide over each other.

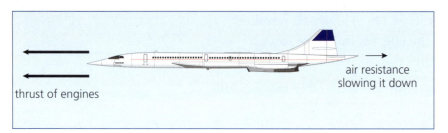

thrust of engines

air resistance slowing it down

When a car or a plane has a steady speed, the forces of friction are balancing the driving force.

Brakes use friction to slow down a car. The greater the speed of the car:

- the greater the braking force needed to slow down the car in the same time; or
- the longer it takes the car to slow down if you use the same braking force.

If you brake too hard then the car will skid. This is because the tyres lose their grip on the road – there is not enough friction between the tyres and the road.

When a car slows down, friction causes the tyres (and the brake pads) to heat up. It also wears the tread on the tyres so they need replacing (or they become dangerous and illegal).

Cover the page, then write down the name of the force that slows down moving things. Check your answer.

Friction causes objects to heat up and to wear away at their surfaces.

The stopping distance of a car depends on:

■ the distance the car travels while the driver thinks

■ the distance the car travels while the brakes work.

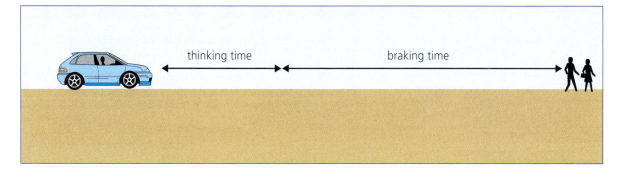

It takes longer to stop a car if:

■ the car is travelling faster

■ the driver's reactions are slowed down (for example, tiredness, drink or drugs)

■ the road conditions are poor (for example, it is wet, icy or there is poor visibility)

■ the car is not in a roadworthy condition (for example, worn brakes).

The faster an object moves through air or water, the greater the force of friction against it.

When a person falls from an aeroplane:

■ at first the person speeds up because of gravity

■ the force of friction through the air eventually balances the force of gravity

■ the forces are now balanced

■ the person now falls at a constant speed (stops speeding up).

This is called **terminal velocity**.

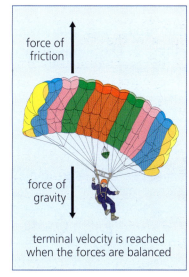

Terminal velocity

Questions

1 Why does a person fall to ground more slowly from an aeroplane when using a parachute?

2 Draw a spider diagram to show the things that would affect how quickly a car stops. Put **car takes longer to stop** at the centre of the diagram.

3 Which **two** forces are balanced when an object falling from the sky reaches terminal velocity?

Earth in space

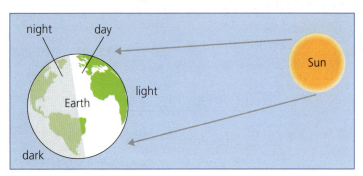

Day and night

The Earth turns around once on its axis every 24 hours.
The half of the Earth facing the Sun is in daylight, in the other half it is night.

It takes the Earth 365 days to orbit the Sun.

Planets and comets

The planets you can see in the night sky look like stars, but they move very slowly against the background of the constellations. This is because the planets, including Earth, move in orbits around the Sun. The further away from the Sun a planet is, the longer it takes to make one complete orbit.

The orbits of the planets are squashed circles (called ellipses). The Sun is quite close to the centre of all these orbits.

Constellations are the patterns made by the positions of the stars in the night sky (for example, the Plough, Orion's belt).

Planets do not give out their own light. We see them because they reflect light from the Sun.

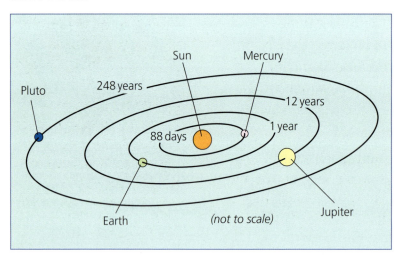

Planets orbit the Sun

Unlike the planets, you can only see comets at certain times. This is because comets have orbits that are far from circular. They are very much closer to the Sun at some times than at other times, and this is when they are visible from Earth.

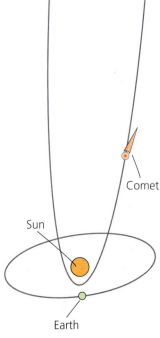

A comet's highly elliptical orbit (not to scale)

Gravity in space

As the Earth orbits the Sun, so the Moon orbits the Earth. Like all bodies, the Earth, Sun and Moon attract each other due the force of **gravity**. As the distance between these bodies gets larger, the force of gravity becomes much less. It becomes disproportionately smaller. In other words, if the distance doubles, the force of gravity is less than half.

A smaller body (for example, the Moon around the Earth) will stay in orbit because of the combination of high speed and the force of gravity.

satellite too slow – falls to Earth

satellite too fast – goes off into space

satellite correct speed – stays in orbit

(not to scale)

Staying in orbit

Satellites

Satellites stay in orbit for the same reason as the planets – a combination of high speed and the force of gravity. To stay in orbit at a particular distance from the Earth, satellites must move at a particular speed.

Communication satellites (such as those used for television) are in orbit high above the equator. They move at the same speed as the Earth so that they always in the same place above the Earth. This is called a **geostationary orbit**. No more that 400 of these satellites can be put into orbit at any one time, otherwise they would interfere with the each other's signals.

Satellites are used to:
* send information between places a long way apart
* look at conditions across the planet, such as weather
* look at the Universe without our atmosphere getting in the way.

Monitoring satellites are used to scan the Earth to see what is going on. They are put into a low orbit over the poles (a **polar orbit**). As the Earth spins beneath them, they can scan the Earth once a day.

Questions

1. The Hubble telescope orbits the Earth. How is it able to do this?
2. The Hubble telescope is able to take much clearer pictures of space than we can take from Earth. Suggest a reason for this.
3. What type of orbit are communication satellites placed and why are they placed there?

The universe

Our Sun is only one of many millions of stars in a group called the Milky Way. The Milky Way is a **galaxy**.

The stars in the Milky Way are millions of times further away than the planets in our solar system – a very long way off!

The Universe is made up of billions of galaxies just like our Milky Way, and galaxies are often many millions of times further apart than stars in a galaxy.

The Universe is really so big it is impossible to imagine it.

The life history of a star

Stars, including the Sun, form when enough dust and gas from space is pulled together by gravitational attraction. Smaller masses also form. They are attracted by a larger mass (like the Sun). They become planets in orbit. Because stars are so massive:

■ the force of gravity tends to draw the matter together

■ the very high temperatures tend to make the star expand.

During the **stable** period (which may last for billions of years) these forces are balanced. Our Sun is at this stage in its life. However, the forces of expansion then begin to 'win' and the star expands and becomes a **red giant**. It now becomes so big that the forces of expansion decrease and the force of gravity becomes the stronger force.

The star now contracts under its own gravity to become a **white dwarf**. Its matter may be millions of times denser than that of Earth. If the red giant is massive enough it may rapidly contact and then explode to become a **supernova**. Dust and gas are thrown into space and a very dense **neutron star** remains.

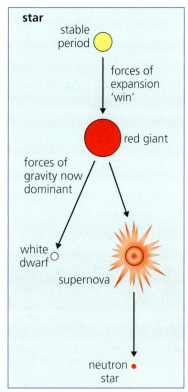

The life history of a star

Is there life out there?

People have always wanted to know if there is life on other planets in our solar system or around other stars. There are three ways of trying to find out.

■ We may be able to see living organisms such as microorganisms by going, for example to Mars or Europa (a moon of Jupiter). Robots can be used to send pictures or collect samples. These collections may show fossilised remains.

■ Living organisms cause changes in the atmosphere. On Earth, for example, plants produce a large amount of oxygen. If we could detect similar changes in other atmospheres on other planets, and show that they were nothing to do with geology or other chemical reactions, then this would suggest that living organisms have been present.

■ We might be able to detect signals or communicate with other life forms that have technologies as advanced as our own. The search for extra-terrestrial intelligence (SETI) has used radio telescopes to try to detect meaningful signals (not just 'noise') for more than 40 years.

None of these methods has yet given us any proof of life in other places, but the search continues.

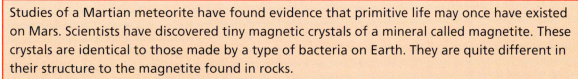

Studies of a Martian meteorite have found evidence that primitive life may once have existed on Mars. Scientists have discovered tiny magnetic crystals of a mineral called magnetite. These crystals are identical to those made by a type of bacteria on Earth. They are quite different in their structure to the magnetite found in rocks.

These scientists claim it is not possible to produce this type of crystal in any way other than by bacteria, so this proves there were once bacteria on Mars. Other scientists are not so sure!

Questions

1 How do stars and planets form?

2 What is a red giant?

3 NASA is sending a new 'rover' robot to Mars to detect and analyse minerals and water samples. What could these samples tell us about life on Mars?

Transferring energy

Work done

When a force moves an object work is done. If you carry a bag across a room then work has been done.

Work is done by transferring energy from one object to another. You can calculate the work done using this formula:

J = joule
N = newton
m = metre

work done (J) = **force applied** (N) × **distance moved** (m)

> **Worked example**
>
> **Q** Chris moves a bag of potatoes weighing 50 N a distance of 20 m. How much work has he done?
>
> **A** work done = force × distance
> = 50 × 20
> = 1000 J (remember the units)

Heat energy

Energy transferred (work done) against a frictional force usually takes the form of heat.

If you rub two sticks together, friction between the sticks and the energy you transfer cause the sticks to heat up and eventually catch on fire.

In physics, 'work done' means that energy has been transferred from one object to another.

Elastic energy

If you stretch a spring or a piece of elastic:

- before you let it go it has (elastic) **potential energy** – the ability to do work

- if you let it go it has (elastic) **kinetic energy**.

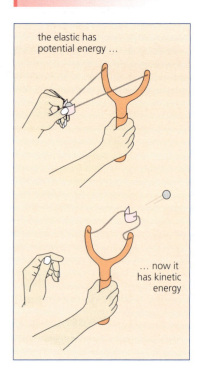

the elastic has potential energy …

… now it has kinetic energy

>
>
> ## Questions
>
> 1 Joanna carries her school bag to school. It weighs 200 N. Joanna carries the bag 450 m. How much work has she done?
>
> 2 What is elastic energy?

Terminal exam questions

1 A car sets off on a journey.

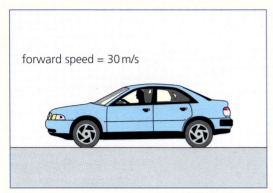

forward speed = 30 m/s

a i It travels 1800 m in 80 s. What is its
average speed? [3]

ii At one point the car accelerates
from 30 m/s to 45 m/s. This takes the
car 3 s. What is the car's acceleration
(m/s^2)? [3]

[6 marks]

2 a Samantha has a mass of 50 kg.
Use the information below to work out
her weight. [2]

**weight = mass × gravitational
field strength**

**gravitational field strength on
Earth is 10 N/kg**

b Samantha's bag weighs 120 N. She
moves her bag over a distance of 15 m.
How much work has she done? [3]

[5 marks]

3 a You travel into town on your bike.
You cycle 1200 metres and take
200 seconds to complete the journey.
What is your average speed? [3]

b You start off at rest. After 10 seconds
your speed is 5 m/s.
What is your acceleration? [3]

c Name **one** force which is stopping you
accelerating any faster. [1]

[7 marks]

4 a Give **three** uses of satellites. [3]

b How do satellites manage to stay
in orbit? [2]

[5 marks]

5 This is a distance-time graph of a
car journey.

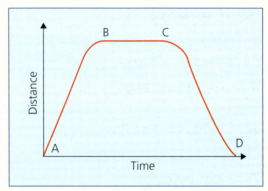

a Between which two points is the
car travelling away from the starting
point? [2]

b Between which two points is the car
stationary (not moving)? [2]

c At which point has the car returned to
where it started? [1]

[5 marks]

Total for test: 28 marks

Making waves

It is easy to make waves in ropes, swings and across the surface of water (for example, ripples on the surface of a pond).

What are waves?

A wave is a regular pattern of disturbances. It moves energy from one place to another without taking any substance with it. So, for example, a wave travelling through a metal spring does not carry metal from the beginning to the end of the spring.

Measuring waves

- The 'height' of a wave is called its **amplitude**.
- The distance between one point on a wave and the same point on the next is called the **wavelength**.
- The number of waves passing a point per second is the **frequency**. This is measured in hertz (Hz), which is the number of waves per second. For example, 50 Hz is 50 waves per second.
- The speed at which a wave is travelling can be found by:

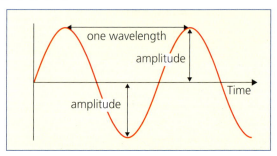

Measuring a wave

wave speed (m/s) = frequency (Hz) × wavelength (m)

Worked example

Q A wave has a speed of 50 m/s and a frequency of 10 hertz. What is the wavelength of the wave?

A wavelength $= \dfrac{\text{wave speed}}{\text{frequency}}$

$= \dfrac{50}{10} = 5 \text{ m}$

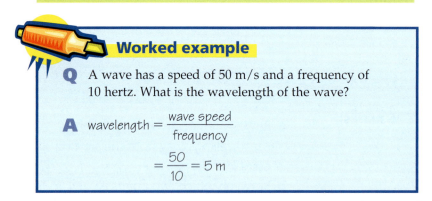

Measuring pitch

The larger the amplitude the louder the sound.

Pitch is a measure of the frequency of sound waves. A high-pitched sound has a greater frequency than a low-pitched sound.

Types of wave movement

These are two types of wave movement.

Transverse waves

The disturbances in transverse waves travel at right angles to the direction that the wave is travelling. This is what you probably imagine when you think of a wave. Waves through water and rope travel this way. Light waves are also transverse waves. They can travel through a vacuum.

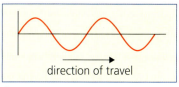
direction of travel

A transverse wave

Longitudinal waves

The disturbances are in the direction of travel. This is the way that waves travel through springs. It is also the way that sound waves travel through solids, liquids and gases.

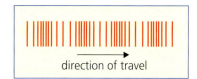
direction of travel

A longitudinal wave

Viewing waves

The **oscilloscope** is a piece of equipment for showing vibrations as waves. For example, a tuning fork makes vibrations. We hear the vibrations as sound. The oscilloscope shows the vibrations as a wave.

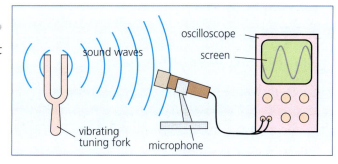
Sound waves show up on an oscilloscope

Ultrasound

Electronic systems can be used to produce **ultrasonic waves**. They are called ultrasonic because we cannot hear them. They are too high pitched.

These ultrasonic waves can be used:

- in industry for cleaning and quality control
- to check on a baby's development in the womb.

Questions

1 Look at the four diagrams of sound waves. Which shows the wave with:

   a the highest frequency

   b the longest wavelength

   c the greatest amplitude?

2 Give **one** example of a transverse wave, and **one** example of a longitudinal wave

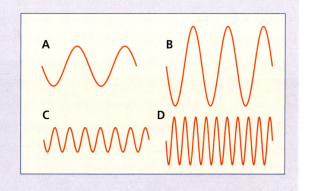

How waves behave

Reflection

Just as waves travelling across the surface of water can be reflected, so too can light and sound waves.

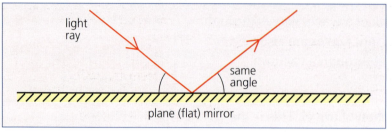

The reflection of light

Reflection is the bouncing of waves from a hard surface.
Echoes are sound waves reflected off hard surfaces.
When a **light** ray hits a shiny surface like a mirror, it leaves the surface of the mirror at the same angle.

Refraction

Waves travelling across the surface of water can also be refracted. This happens when the water becomes either shallower or deeper.

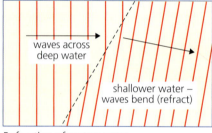

Refraction of water waves

Light waves also refract:

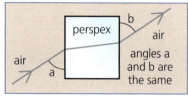
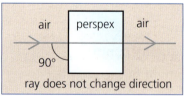

Refraction of light rays through a perspex block

Refraction is the bending of waves as they pass from one substance to another. This is because the substances have different densities. A light ray bends as it passes from air, through a perspex block and back to air again.
If a light ray passes into another substance along the normal (at right angles to it), the light does not refract.

If you pass white light through a prism the light splits into different colours, because each colour is refracted to a different extent. This results in a spectrum that has the same colours in the same order as a rainbow.

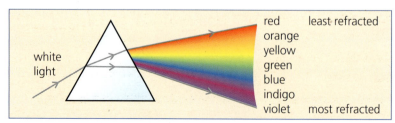

Refraction of light through a prism

White light is made up of many different wavelengths of light, each a different colour. When white light passes through a prism, a spectrum of these colours is produced. This is because the light waves are refracted by different amounts.

Internal reflection

When a ray of light travels from glass, perspex or water into air then some of the light is also reflected at the boundary.

air most light refracted
glass block
ray of light
some light relected internally

Internal reflection

Diffraction

When a wave moves through a gap or spreads out as it passes an obstacle, the wave spreads out from the edges. This is called **diffraction**. Waves having a longer wavelength are more strongly diffracted.

Electromagnetic radiation and sound can be diffracted. This supports the idea that they travel as waves.

Electromagnetic radiation is explained on the next page.

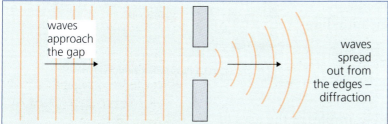
waves approach the gap

waves spread out from the edges – diffraction

Diffraction

It is because of diffraction that:

- sounds may be heard in the shadow of buildings (around corners)
- radio signals can sometimes be picked up in the shadow of hills.

Shock waves

We cannot see inside the Earth. Our knowledge of how it is made up comes from studying the shock waves from earthquakes. These are called **seismic waves** and are detected using seismographs.

The layers of the Earth are substances with different densities. As seismic waves travel through the Earth, they are **refracted** through these substances.

Questions

1. Look at these diagrams then answer the questions.

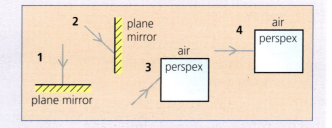

   a. Draw diagrams of how light rays 1 and 2 will reflect.

   b. Draw diagrams of how light rays 3 and 4 will refract.

2. Explain why you can hear someone calling you from around the corner of a building.

Electromagnetic radiation

Light is only one form of **electromagnetic radiation**. But what *is* electromagnetic radiation? The answer is – waves that can pass at the same speed through space (that is, through a vacuum).

There is a continuous spectrum of electromagnetic radiation. We cannot see most of it. Different types of electromagnetic radiation have different frequencies and wavelengths.

These different forms of electromagnetic radiation are all absorbed or transmitted in different ways by:

- different substances; and
- different types of surface.

On these two pages you will find examples of the uses of different types of radiation.

When radiation is absorbed by a substance the energy it carries:

- makes the substance hotter
- may create an alternating electric current with the same frequency as the radiation itself (this is how a television works).

highest frequency	shortest wavelength
gamma rays	
X-rays	
ultraviolet rays	
light	
infra red rays	
microwaves	
radio waves	
lowest frequency	longest wavelength

The spectrum of electromagnetic radiation

Cover the page, then write down **three** types of electromagnetic radiation.
Check your answer.

Using electromagnetic radiation

The effects and uses of the different types of radiation depend on their various properties.

Radio waves

These are used to transmit radio and TV programmes all over the Earth. The longer wavelength radio waves are reflected back to Earth from an electrically charged layer in the Earth's upper atmosphere. This means that the waves can be sent around the Earth, even though it is a sphere.

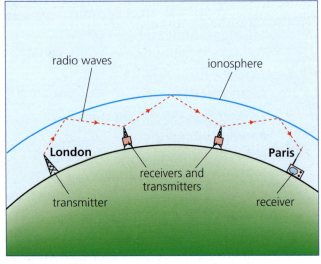

The transmission of radiowaves

Microwaves

These can easily pass through the Earth's atmosphere. They are therefore used to pass information to and receive information from satellites and within mobile phone networks. Microwave radiation (with wavelengths strongly absorbed by water particles) is used in microwave cookers for cooking food or heating drinks.

A microwave oven

Infra red radiation

This is used in grills, toasters and radiant heaters (like electric fires). It is also used to carry telephone messages along optical fibres and for TV and remote video controls.

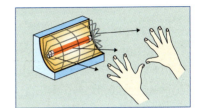

An electric fire

Visible light

Doctors use endoscopes to look inside people. Endoscopes work by sending light down optical fibres (fine glass tubes). The light stays inside the fibres and doesn't come out until it reaches the end. The light stays in the fibre because it is reflected from side to side and so is 'bounced' all the way down to the end.

This is called **total internal reflection**. It happens when the light hits the inside of the fibre at an angle greater than an angle that is called the 'critical angle'.

In an endoscope, some bundles of fibres carry the light down into the patient's body. Other bundles carry the light reflected from inside the body back up into the doctor's eye. These are called **optical fibres**.

Optical fibres are now also used for carrying cable TV and some telephone calls. The fibres can also be used to carry light to illuminate car dashboards.

They can carry more information than electrical signals down a cable of the same size.

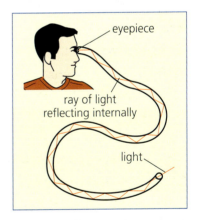

Using an endoscope

Questions

1. Arrange these four types of radiation in order. Put the type with longest wavelength first, and the type with the shortest wavelength last.

   ultraviolet rays   microwaves   gamma rays   X-rays

2. Astronauts cannot shout at each other through space on a space walk. Why does this tell you that sound is not a type of electromagnetic radiation?

More electromagnetic radiation

Ultraviolet radiation

This is used to make white people go 'brown' on sun beds. Special coatings that absorb UV radiation and emit it well are used both in fluorescent lamps and for security coding.

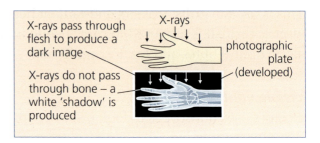

UV light

X radiation

X radiation (X-rays) does not pass easily through some materials (for example, bone). It is used to make shadow pictures. Pictures can be made of broken bones or cracks inside metal structures (for example, bridges).

X-rays pass through flesh to produce a dark image

X-rays do not pass through bone – a white 'shadow' is produced

X-rays

photographic plate (developed)

Gamma radiation

This is used to:

- kill harmful bacteria in food
- sterilise surgical instruments
- kill cancer cells.

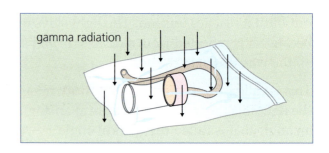

gamma radiation

Dangers of radiation

Type of radiation	Dangers of exposure	How to reduce exposure
Microwaves	Absorbed by water in living cells. Causes the cells to heat up and be killed or damaged	Make sure that the seals around the door are good.
Infra red radiation	Absorbed by the skin and felt as heat	Do not stay in the Sun too long
Ultraviolet radiation	Passes through the skin to deeper tissues. High doses can cause cells to become cancerous	Darker skins have natural UV protection. Wearing UV filter sun lotions can help reduce the risks of sunburn and damage to skin
X-rays	Mostly go straight through the skin and soft tissues, but some absorbed by cells. High doses can kill cells. Low doses can cause cells to become cancerous	If taking X-rays, stay well away from the source. As a patient, you should not be X-rayed too often
Gamma rays	Mostly go straight through the skin and soft tissues, but some absorbed by cells. High doses can kill cells. Low doses can cause cells to become cancerous	Enclose the source in a thick, lead-lined container

Analogue and digital signals ● ● ● ● ● ● ● ● ●

Speech and music can be converted into electrical signals. These signals can be carried long distances through cables, or by using electromagnetic waves as carriers. This is how most televisions and radios work.

Information can also be converted into light or infra red signals and sent along optical fibres.
But how are these signals different?

Analogue signals vary in amplitude and frequency, just like speech and music. This is why you have to 'tune' your television or radio to receive particular frequencies (BBC Radio 1 is 97.6–99.8 FM)

Digital signals are coded as a series of pulses. There is no variation in amplitude or frequency. The signal is either on or off.

Digital signals have advantages:

■ they have a higher quality – there is no change in them as they are transmitted

■ more information can be sent at the same time – whether it is through cable, optic fibre or carrier wave.

Digital television and radio are gradually replacing analogue. They can offer many more programmes at the same time, and the quality of the sound or picture is much better.

Questions

1 Copy and complete the table using these words:

X-rays
infra red
radio waves
ultraviolet

Type of radiation	Use
	TV remote controls
	transmit information
	sun-beds
	take pictures of fractures

2 Why are X-rays used to show broken bones?

3 Name **one** type of useful electromagnetic radiation. Describe its use and how it might be harmful.

4 Why do digital signals result in a clearer picture on a TV screen?

Radioactive substances

These are substances that give out radiation all of the time. They are all around us in the air, building materials and food. Radiation also reaches us from space. This is all called **background radiation**.

There are various sorts of radiation, including:

- **alpha** (α) radiation – easily absorbed by a few centimetres of air or a thin sheet of paper
- **beta** (β) radiation – passes through paper but is absorbed by a thin sheet of metal
- **gamma** (γ) radiation – very penetrating, it needs a few centimetres of lead or several metres of concrete to stop the rays.

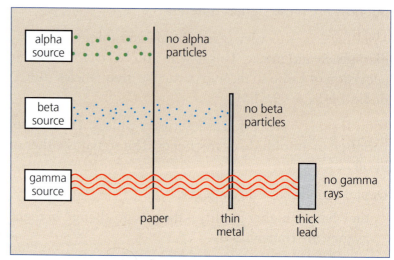

What does radiation do?

Causing and killing cancer

If radiation bumps into neutral atoms or molecules these may become charged ions.

When radiation ionises molecules in living cells it can cause damage, which may result in cancer. The bigger the dose of radiation you have, the higher the chances of getting cancer.

Very high doses of radiation can kill cells. They are used to kill cancer cells and harmful microorganisms such as bacteria.

Testing thickness

As radiation is absorbed by different thicknesses of various substances it can be used to test them in industry. For example, alpha radiation is used to test the thickness of paper as it is manufactured.

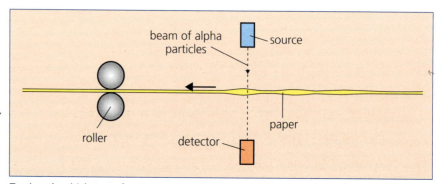

Testing the thickness of paper

Dangers from radiation

How dangerous?	When sources are outside the body	When sources are inside the body
Most dangerous	Beta and gamma radiation – can reach the cells of organs and damage them	Alpha radiation – strongly absorbed by cells
Least dangerous	Alpha radiation – unlikely to reach living cells	Beta and gamma radiation – less likely to be absorbed by cell

Workers at risk from radiation wear a special badge to check the amount of radiation they have been exposed to. The more the exposure, the darker the photographic film in the badge becomes.

Understanding radioactivity

Before you can understand how radioactive substances give out radiation, you need to understand the structure of atoms.

The structure of the atom

Alpha and beta radiation is caused by changes in the nucleus of an atom.

Atoms have a small nucleus made up from **protons** and **neutrons**. **Electrons** move around the nucleus.

The mass and charge for each are shown in the table.

There are always the same number of protons and electrons in an atom. This means that an atom as a whole has no electrical charge. The number of protons and neutrons together is known as the **mass number**.

	Mass	Charge
proton	1	+1
neutron	1	0
electron	hardly anything	−1

All the atoms in an element have the same number of protons – the **proton number** (for example, sodium always has 11 protons). But the number of neutrons in the atoms of an element might vary. Atoms of an element with different numbers of neutrons are known as **isotopes**.

Radioactive isotopes

These have unstable nuclei that break down quite readily. When the nucleus breaks down (disintegrates):

■ it gives out (emits) radiation

■ a different atom is left with a different number of protons.

This is how alpha and beta radiation are produced.

The older the radioactive material, the less radiation it emits. We use this idea to find out how old things are (for example, rocks).

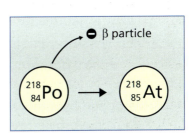

Radioactive polonium becomes astatine as it breaks down

Understanding radioactivity continued

Discovering the atom

An early idea of the atom was the 'plum pudding model'. Scientists described the atom as like a positively charged sphere with negative electrons studded throughout it, like raisins in a pudding.

In 1911 Ernest Rutherford carried out an experiment in which he fired alpha particles at a very thin piece of gold foil. Most went straight through, and only a few were scattered at wide angles by the foil. This was a surprise because, as in the plum pudding model, he expected the particles to bounce off the positively charged spheres of the atoms.

Rutherford concluded that most of an atom was empty space, with a tiny nucleus. If an atom was the size of a school hall its nucleus would be the size of a full stop! This work led to our present idea of the atom.

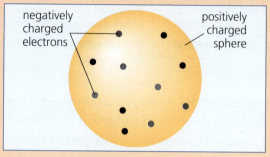

The 'plum pudding' model of an atom

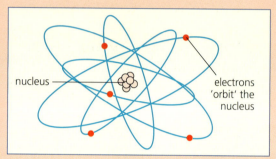

The structure of an atom

Half-life

The **half-life** of a radioactive source is the time taken for the number of radioactive atoms to half. In other words, for the substance to become half as radioactive.

For example, the half-life of substance X = 100 years:

■ after 50 years it is half as radioactive

■ after another 50 years it has lost another half of it radioactivity and is only 25% as radioactive as when it was formed.

The graph shows this.

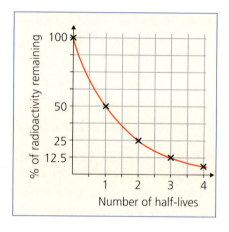

Questions

1 Why is gamma radiation not used in testing the thickness of paper?

2 Copy and complete the sentences using these words:

   alpha   background   gamma   beta

   _____ radiation will pass through a metre of concrete. _____ radiation is stopped by a thin sheet of paper. _____ radiation passes through paper but is stopped by a few centimetres of metal. _____ radiation is the radiation that reaches us from space as well as from some natural minerals.

Terminal exam questions

1 Copy this diagram of a wave.

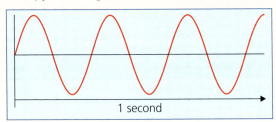

1 second

a i Mark on the diagram **one** wavelength. [1]

ii What is the frequency of the wave? [1]

b These diagrams show **two** different sound waves, A and B.

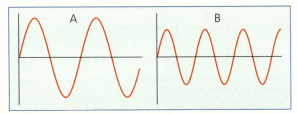

A   B

i Which of the waves shows the loudest sound? Explain your answer. [2]

ii Which sound has the highest pitch? Explain your answer. [2]

c i Copy and complete the diagram of a light ray passing through a glass block. [3]

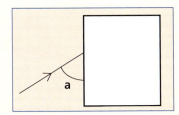

a

ii What is meant by 'refraction'? [1]

iii What causes the refraction of a wave? [1]

[11 marks]

2 a Copy and complete the diagram to show how white light is split up by a prism. (You need to show only red and blue light) [3]

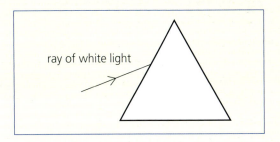

ray of white light

b Visible light is one form of electromagnetic radiation. What is electromagnetic radiation? [2]

c Copy and complete the spectrum of electromagnetic radiation. Use words from this list to match the spaces 1–4. [4]

X-rays   **infra red**

visible light   **radio waves**

highest frequency   gamma rays
                                  1
                           ultraviolet
                                  2
                                  3
                           microwaves
lowest frequency   4

d Match the type of radiation with its uses as shown in the table. Use words from the list. [4]

X-rays   **microwaves**

infra red   **ultraviolet**

	Use
1	used to make toast (for example, in a toaster)
2	used to transmit to satellites
3	used with sunbeds
4	used to photograph broken bones

e What is meant by 'total internal reflection'? [1]

[14 marks]

Total for test: 25 marks

Answers to module test and terminal exam questions

Humans as organisms

Question	Answer	Marks	Total
1	1 red cells 2 plasma 3 platelets 4 white cells	1 1 1 1	 4
2	1 trachea 2 bronchus 3 air sac 4 rib	1 1 1 1	 4
3	1 A 2 D 3 C 4 C	1 1 1 1	 4

Question	Answer	Marks	Total
4	C and E	2	2
5	A and D	2	2
6	1. B 2. C 3. D 4. A	1 1 1 1	 4
7	1. B 2. A 3. D 4. B	1 1 1 1	 4

Total for test: 24 marks

Maintenance of life

Question	Answer	Marks	Total
1	1 chloroplast 2 nucleus 3 cell wall 4 cytoplasm	1 1 1 1	 4
2	1 stomata 2 guard cells 3 xylem 4 phloem	1 1 1 1	 4
3	1 nose 2 ear 3 tongue 4 skin	1 1 1 1	 4
4	1 cell wall 2 nucleus 3 cytoplasm 4 cell membrane	1 1 1 1	 4

Question	Answer	Marks	Total
5	B and D	2	2
6	B and E	2	2
7	1. A 2. C 3. D 4. B	1 1 1 1	 4
8	1. B 2. C 3. A 4. D	1 1 1 1	 4

Total for test: 28 marks

Environment

Question			Answer	Marks	Total
1	a	i	*Any two from:* • temperature • amount of light/sun • amount of water • availability of carbon dioxide/oxygen.	2	
		ii	*Any two from:* • amount of food/bushes to eat • number of voles to eat them • number of small birds to eat them *or two of the first list if not used in part **i** (excluding amount of sunlight).*	2	
	b	i	It will decrease as not enough caterpillars to eat.	2	
		ii	The population is likely to decrease as the owls will be forced to eat more voles.	2	**8 marks**
2	a	i	Carbon dioxide.	1	
		ii	**Any two from:** • in sugars • in starch • in proteins • in fats.	2	

	b		*Any two from:*
			• by the plant
			  through respiration or
			• eaten by animal
			  then through respiration or
			• eaten by animal that dies
			  decomposes/bacteria break it down
			  through respiration.
				4	

	c		Sewage works compost heaps.	1 1	**9 marks**
3	a	i	*Any two from:* • increasing cars/burning of fossil fuels • increasing number of people • increasing industry/need for electricity/power stations.	2	
		ii	*Any two from:* • increased building • dumping waste • quarrying • farming.	2	
	b		*Any three from:* • sewage in water • fertiliser in water • chemicals in water • smoke in air • sulphur dioxide in air • carbon dioxide in air		

continued

Environment *continued*

Question			Answer	Marks	Total
3b *cont.*			• pesticides on land • herbicides (weedkillers) on land. *There are many answers – these are from the syllabus. You will get marks for all correct answers, whether on the syllabus or not. This is the same for all questions where you may write down correct answers not on the syllabus, so long as they are good science.*	3	**7 marks**
4	**a**	**i**	Water plants.	1	
		ii	Pike.	1	
		iii	Either water beetles or tadpoles.	1	
	b		Any two from: • space • food • hiding places.	2	
	c		It shows the amount of mass available in the food chain or, better still, the amount of energy at each level.	1	**6 marks**

Total for test: 30 marks

Inheritance and selection

Question			Answer	Marks	Total
1	**a**		**1** nucleus **2** chromosomes **3** genes **4** alleles	4	
	b	**i**	To produce new plants.	1	
		ii	Environmental reasons (for example, nutrients, water or light).	1	
		iii	Any two from: • warmth • water • nutrients • light.	2	**8 marks**
2	**a**	**i**	Cell membranes.	1	
		ii	Only if both parents are carriers or have the disorder.	1 1	
	b	**i**	Affects the nervous system.	1	
		ii	In chromosomes/genes only one parent needs to have the disorder.	1 1	**6 marks**
3	**a**		A part of a chromosome that controls a specific characteristic, for example, eye colour.	2	
	b		One of two different forms of genes, for example, blue eye colour	2	
	c		A dominant gene masks the effect of a recessive gene. Both alleles must be recessive if the recessive characteristic is to show.	2	**6 marks**

Question			Answer	Marks	Total
4	a	i	Any two from: • select male and female • with good characteristics • reproduce from them.	2	
		ii	Produce young with wanted characteristics.	1 1	
	b	i	Stop eggs being released.	1 1	
		ii	Stimulate/encourage egg production.	1 1	8 marks
5	a		Asexual.	1	
	b		Produced by cell division for growth (mitosis) they have exactly the same genes as the parent.	1 1	
	c		Take male sex cells from a plant that has bigger strawberries and use them to fertilise female sex cells from another plant with large strawberries. Grow the seed you produce. This is known as selective breeding.	2	5 marks

Total for test: 33 marks

Metals

Question	Answer	Marks	Total
1	1 strong acid 2 weak acid 3 neutral 4 weak alkali	1 1 1 1	4
2	1 neutralisation 2 reduction 3 oxidation 4 displacement	1 1 1 1	4
3	1 metal chloride 2 metal oxide 3 hydrogen 4 metal hydroxide or oxide	1 1 1 1	4
4	1 aluminium 2 carbon 3 iron 4 gold	1 1 1 1	4

Question	Answer	Marks	Total
5	A and E	2	2
6	A and E	2	2
7	1 A 2 B 3 B 4 C	1 1 1 1	4
8	A and C	2	2
9	1 B 2 A 3 D 4 C	1 1 1 1	4

Total for test: 30 marks

Earth materials

Question	Answer	Marks	Total
1	1 concrete	1	
	2 calcium carbonate	1	
	3 quicklime	1	
	4 slaked lime	1	4
2	1 bitumen	1	
	2 gasoline	1	
	3 kerosene	1	
	4 fuel oil	1	4
3	1 oxygen	1	
	2 carbon dioxide	1	
	3 sulphur dioxide	1	
	4 nitrogen	1	4

Question	Answer	Marks	Total
4	B and C	2	2
5	A and E	2	2
6	A and E	2	2
7	1. A	1	
	2. B	1	
	3. D	1	
	4. B	1	4
8	1. C	1	
	2. D	1	
	3. D	1	
	4. D	1	4

Total for test: 26 marks

Patterns of chemical change

Question		Answer	Marks	Total
1	a	Beer and alcohol.	2	
	b	Lactose sugar is turned into lactic acid.	2	
	c	The enzymes that carry out these reactions in yeast and bacteria are destroyed at temperatures greater than 45 °C.	6	6 marks

2	a	Any three methods for 3 marks each:
		• heat –
		  particles move faster
		  bump into each other more often/bump into each other with more energy
		• more concentrated –
		  bump into each other more often
		  particles closer together
		• greater surface area –
		  more particles
		  bump into each other more often
		• increase the pressure –
		  particles bump into each other more often and with greater energy, only in a gas.
		• catalyst –
		  lowers the activation energy
			max 9	

	b	The least amount of energy necessary for a reaction to work.	1 1	11 marks

Question			Answer	Marks	Total
3	**a**	**i**	1 Nitrogen or hydrogen 2 hydrogen or nitrogen 3 oxygen 4 nitric acid.	4	
		ii	450 °C 200 atmospheres	2	
		iii	Iron.	1	
	b		It may run off the land into rivers/lakes/ponds when it rains and get into drinking water.	1 1 1 1	
	c		A reaction that takes in energy/heat.	1 1	**13 marks**

4	**a**	**i**	CH_3COOH: $2 \times C = 24$ *for 1 mark*
			                 $4 \times H = 4$ *for 1 mark*
			                 $2 \times O = \underline{32}$ *for 1 mark*
			                     60 *for 1 mark*
				4	

		ii	$Ca(OH)_2$: $1 \times Ca = 40$ *for 1 mark*
			             $2 \times O = 32$ *for 1 mark*
			             $2 \times H = \underline{2}$ *for 1 mark*
			                 74 *for 1 mark*
				4	

	b	**i**	Water is H_2O
			M_r is: $O = 16$
			          $2 \times H = \underline{2}$
			               18 *for 1 mark*
			$\%O = \dfrac{16}{18} \times 100$ *for 1 mark*
			   $= 88.9\%$ *for 1 mark*
				3	

		ii	Calcium carbonate is $CaCO_3$
			M_r is: $Ca = 40$
			            $C = 12$
			         $3 \times O = \underline{48}$
			               100 *for 1 mark*
			$\%C = \dfrac{12}{100} \times 100$ *for 1 mark*
			   $= 12\%$ *for 1 mark*
				3	**14 marks**

Total for test: 44 marks

Structures and bonding

Question			Answer	Marks	Total
1	a	i	11	1	
		ii	11	1	
		iii	12	1	
		iv	23	1	
	b		2 electrons in inner shell 8 electrons in next shell 1 electron in the outer shell (1 mark off for each mistake)	2	
	c	i	Fluorine completed as 2, 7 one electron moves from potassium the electron moves to fluorine.	3	
		ii	Ionic.	1	**10 marks**
2	a	i	Second column shaded.	1	
		ii	Any two from: • hydrogen • lithium • sodium • potassium.	2	
		iii	Fluorine chlorine.	1 1	
	b		There are 8 electrons in the full outer shell so it is very difficult to lose or gain electrons.	1 1	**7 marks**
3	a	i	39	1	
		ii	19	1	
		iii	20	1	
	b			3	
	c	i		3	
		ii	Ionic	1	
		iii	An ion is an atom with more or less electrons than protons. It is a charged particle.	1 1	
		iv	Lithium loses its outer electron. to become a positively charged ion.	1 1	**14 marks**

Total for test: 31 marks

Energy

Question	Answer	Marks	Total
1	**1** convection **2** insulation **3** conduction **4** radiation	1 1 1 1	4
2	**1** W **2** J **3** s **4** kWh	1 1 1 1	4
3	**1** food mixer **2** radio **3** toaster **4** torch	1 1 1 1	4
4	**1** uranium **2** coal **3** hydroelectric **4** solar	1 1 1 1	4

Question	Answer	Marks	Total
5	**C** and **D**	2	2
6	**B** and **E**	2	2
7	1. **B** 2. **D** 3. **B** 4. **A**	1 1 1 1	4
8	1. **C** 2. **B** 3. **B** 4. **C**	1 1 1 1	4

Total for test: 28 marks

Electricity

Question	Answer	Marks	Total
1	**1** diode **2** fuse **3** resistor **4** thermistor	1 1 1 1	4
2	**1** green/yellow wire **2** blue wire **3** fuse **4** brown wire	1 1 1 1	4
3	sentence order is **2 4 1 3**	4	4
4	**1** watt **2** hertz **3** ampere **4** volt	1 1 1 1	4

Question	Answer	Marks	Total
5	**B** and **D**	2	2
6	**D** and **E**	2	2
7	1. **C** 2. **C** 3. **A** 4. **D**	1 1 1 1	4
8	1. **A** 2. **B** 3. **D** 4. **B**	1 1 1 1	4

Total for test: 28 marks

Forces

Question			Answer	Marks	Total
1	a	i	speed = $\dfrac{\text{distance}}{\text{time}}$	1	
			$= \dfrac{1800}{80}$	1	
			$= 22.5 \, \text{m/s}$	1	
		ii	acceleration = $\dfrac{\text{change in velocity}}{\text{time}}$	1	
			$= \dfrac{45 - 30}{3}$	1	
			$= 5 \, \text{m/s}^2$	1	6 marks
2	a		$50 \times 10 =$ 500 N	1 1	
	b		work = force $\times$ distance	1	
			$= 120 \times 15$		
			$= 1800$	1	
			J	1	5 marks
3	a		speed $= \dfrac{\text{distance}}{\text{time}}$	1	
			$= \dfrac{1200}{200}$		
			$= 6$	1	
			m/s	1	
	b		acceleration $= \dfrac{\text{change in speed}}{\text{time}}$	1	
			$= \dfrac{5}{10}$		
			$= 0.5$	1	
			m/s^2	1	
	c		friction (*or suitable explanation*)	1	7 marks
4	a		Observe the Universe observe weather conditions send information across the planet. *Note: there are other answers that are correct* *(for example, observe other countries).*	1 1 1	
	b		A combination of high speed and the force of gravity.	1 1	5 marks
5	a		A and B	2	
	b		B and C	2	
	c		D	1	5 marks

Total for test: 28 marks

Waves and radiation

Question			Answer	Marks	Total
1	a	i	From one peak to another	1	
		ii	3 (hertz or cycles per second) – this means 3 complete waves pass each second	1	
	b	i	A (no mark unless reason given)	1	
			because the wave has the biggest amplitude (the peaks are bigger)	1	
		ii	B (no mark unless reason given)	1	
			because the frequency is higher (waves closer together)	1	
	c	i			
			Plus 1 extra mark for showing angles a and b are the same.	3	
		ii	Changing direction or 'bending'	1	
		iii	Changes speed or movement from one type of substance to another or for water – the sea becomes shallower or deeper.	1	**11 marks**
2	a			3	
	b		Any two from: • waves • that transfer energy • can pass through space • do not transfer material.	2	
	c		1 X-rays 2 visible light 3 infra red 4 radio waves	4	
	d		1 infra red 2 microwaves 3 ultraviolet 4 X-rays	4	
	e		Light reflected back within the material.	1	**14 marks**

Total for test: 25 marks

Answers to end of spread questions

These notes accompany the questions that are to be found at the end of each double-page spread. They are not mark schemes as these questions are not the same as those you will find in your final examination.

Humans as Organisms

PAGE 3

1

Type of cell	What it does	How it is adapted
nerve	passes information through the body	very long with connections to many other nerve cells
sperm	swims towards the egg cell	has a long tail
ciliated cell	stops mucus building up on the lining of the windpipe	has hair like structures called cilia
red blood cell	carries oxygen around the body	shaped like a lozenge and has no nucleus

2 Muscular tissue and glandular tissue.

3 Cell membrane, nucleus and cytoplasm.

PAGE 5

1 Salivary glands – carbohydrase; stomach – protease; pancreas – carbohydrase, protease and lipase; small intestine – carbohydrase, protease and lipase.

2

fat in butter
↓
lipase produced in pancreas and small intestine
↓
fatty acids and glycerol in blood

protein in cheese
↓
protease produced in stomach, small intestine and pancreas
↓
amino acids in blood

3 These increase the surface area for absorption of small, soluble food particles.

PAGE 7

1 Oxygen, respire, energy, carbon dioxide, water.

2 The ribs.

3 Increase fitness or ideas about increasing the amount of oxygen exchanged with each breath.

4 The ribs move out and up.

PAGE 9

1

Parts of the blood	What they do	Structure
plasma	carries many substances	liquid
red cells	carry oxygen	no nucleus, contains haemoglobin
white cells	helps fight disease	cell with a nucleus
platelets	help heal cuts	bits of cells, no nucleus

2 To cope with the high blood pressure of the blood being pumped out by the heart.

PAGE 11

1 The spider diagram should include: a complete skin, scabs forming when the skin is cut, our air passages have the surface covered in mucus, white cells to digest bacteria, white cells to produce antibodies, white cells to produce antitoxins.

2 They have a cell wall and no nucleus.

3 The disease organism could be in the droplets sneezed, someone may breathe these droplets in.

Maintenance of life

PAGE 15

1 Cell wall – keeps the cell in shape; chloroplast – containing chlorophyll for photosynthesis; vacuole – containing the cell sap.

2 Carbon dioxide, water, chlorophyll, glucose, oxygen.

3 The grass stops growing as it is so cold (the enzymes work only very slowly when it is cold).

PAGE 17

1 Xylem, water, nutrients, sugars, phloem.

2 A thick, waxy layer on the surface of the leaf; stomata that can close to prevent too much water loss.

3 The diffusion of water molecules.

PAGE 19

1 Hormones, lower, quickly, upwards.

2 Iris – controls the amount of light entering the eye; retina – acts as the receptor for light (it is sensitive to light); optic nerve – takes information to the brain; lens – focuses the light onto the retina.

3 A neurone through which messages are sent to the spinal cord or brain.

PAGE 21

1 Carbon dioxide – lungs; water – lungs, skin and as urine; ions – skin and in urine.

2 The sugar level will go up, insulin will be produced (by the pancreas), this lowers the blood sugar level.

3 Brain and liver.

4 The circulatory system.

5 Alcohol slows the nervous system down.

Environment

PAGE 25

1 More light (so more plants, therefore more small animals for the owls to feed on); more small birds (to eat); more plant growth (so more animals for the owls to feed on).

2 There are likely to be fewer (as more owls to eat them).

3 Any three from: fast; sharp teeth, good eyesight, good sense of smell; streamlined; powerful jaws; any other sensible answer.

4 Most are lost by: being eaten; falling in a shady area or an area that is too dry or wet; being trampled; being killed by disease; any other sensible answer.

PAGE 27

1 Plants → slugs → blackbirds.

2
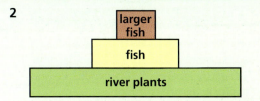

PAGE 29

1 Bacteria, fungi, oxygen, carbon dioxide, decay, respiration.

2 Compost plants and break down sewage.

PAGE 31

1 Building, rubbish tips, raw materials (for example, quarrying for stone), farming.

2 The car is producing nitrogen oxides and sulphur dioxide.

3 Carbon dioxide is a greenhouse gas. Greenhouse gases trap heat in the Earth's atmosphere causing it to become warmer.

Inheritance and selection

PAGE 35

1 Nucleus, chromosomes, genes, alleles.

2 They have exactly the same genes (genetic material).

3 The gene for red petals is dominant.

PAGE 37

1 Warm, wet conditions.

2 They are called genes. They are transferred to bacteria where they will continue to make the same protein. By doing this on a large scale large amounts of protein can be produced for example human insulin.

3 A clone is a new organism produced by asexual reproduction.

PAGE 39

1 A change in the genes of an organism, caused by radiation or some chemicals.

2 An environmental change (for example, temperature, amount of rain), predators may eat them all, disease may kill them all, another species successfully competes against them (for example, eats all of their food).

3 Two of: ionising radiation; radioactive substances; some chemicals.

4 The 'fittest' members of the species survive to breed. Less 'fit' members of the species are less likely to survive and breed.

PAGE 40

1 Hormones; fertility; pituitary gland; secreted.

2 This treatment enables woman to become fertile again. However, it is expensive and multiple births are common.

Metals

PAGE 45

1 Oxygen, hydroxide, hydrochloric acid, hydrogen.

2 Unlike the alkali metals the transition metals have high melting points; are much harder, tougher and stronger; and are less reactive.

PAGE 47

1 Magnesium as it is more reactive than carbon.

2 Reduce; iron; more; carbon monoxide; calcium carbonate; slag.

PAGE 49

1 Oxide, cryolite, negative, positive.

2 So that the different ions are free to move to the electrodes.

3 Na, Al, C, Fe, Au (least reactive).

PAGE 51

1 Potassium sulphate, potassium nitrate, calcium chloride, sodium nitrate.

2 Hydrogen ions (H^+)

Earth materials

PAGE 55

1 From sediment (for example, sand) building up on the sea floor, the weight squeezes water out, the sediment cements together as salts crystallise out.

2 If they are placed under great heat and pressure.

PAGE 57

1 Some seem to 'fit' well together, fossils are similar on continents hundreds of miles apart, there are similar rocks on continents hundreds of miles apart.

2 They float on the mantle, there are convection currents in the mantle, these are caused by heat produced by radioactive processes.

PAGE 59

1 Calcium carbonate, quicklime, slaked lime, cement.

2 The greater the length of the carbon chain the higher the boiling point of the hydrocarbon.

PAGE 61

1 They are heated until they become a gas (vaporise) and are then passed over a catalyst.

2 Water.

PAGE 63

1 Methane, ammonia; carbon dioxide; water vapour.

2 Oxygen has reacted with ammonia to produce nitrogen.

Patterns of chemical change

PAGE 67

1 The particles bump into each other more often as there are more particles in the same space.

2 Increase, collide, greater.

3 The substances reacting will be used up quicker (solids may disappear more quickly), products (for example, gases) will be produced more quickly.

PAGE 69

1 Two from: wine; beer; spirits; yoghurt; cheese; bread.

2 At 30 °C the enzyme still works, at 45 °C the enzyme stops working (the enzyme is damaged by the high temperature).

3 Useful substances would include: alcohol, carbon dioxide and yoghurt.

PAGE 71

1 To work out the M_r of the compound you need to know the A_r of each element making up the compound:

a $CaCO_3$: Ca = 40, C = 12, O = 16 (but there are three of them, so 48)
M_r = 40 + 12 + 48 = 100.

b $MgSO_4$: Mg = 24, S = 32, O = 16 (but there are four of them, so 64)
M_r = 24 + 32 + 64 = 120.

2 a The M_r of sodium chloride is: (Na = 23) +
(Cl = 35) = 58
therefore the proportion of sodium
$= \frac{23}{58} = 39.7\%$.

b The M_r of sulphur dioxide is: (S = 32) +
(O = 16, but there are two of them so 32) = 64
therefore the proportion of sulphur $= \frac{32}{64}$
= 50%.

PAGE 81

1 Iron and platinum.

Structures and bonding

PAGE 75

1 There is always exactly the same number
(protons are positive, electrons are negative
so the charges are balanced).

2 Neutrons.

PAGE 77

1 a 12 **b** 24 **c** 12 **d** 2, 8, 2

2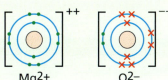

Mg²⁺   O²⁻

3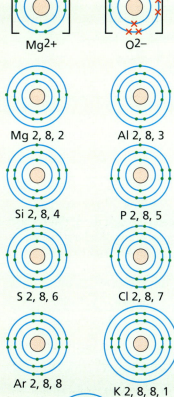

Mg 2, 8, 2   Al 2, 8, 3

Si 2, 8, 4   P 2, 8, 5

S 2, 8, 6   Cl 2, 8, 7

Ar 2, 8, 8   K 2, 8, 8, 1

Ca 2, 8, 8, 2

PAGE 79

1 Atoms, sharing, low.

2 It has the same number of outer electrons.

PAGE 81

1 Any three from: are non-metals; have
coloured vapour as gases; exist as pairs of
atoms (therefore are molecules); form ionic
salts (where the halogen carries one negative
charge); form molecular compounds with
other non-metals.

2 Because the outer (highest energy) shell of
electrons is already full.

3 As it loses one electron to become an ion – it
therefore now has one more proton (positive
charge) in the nucleus than electrons
(negative charge) in the electron shells.

PAGE 83

1 Chloride, positive, electron, chlorine.

2 In photographic film and photographic
paper.

3 The spider should have: chlorine, hydrogen
and sodium hydroxide.

PAGE 85

1 a NaOH **b** MgO **c** Na_2O **d** $MgCl_2$.

2 a Magnesium + oxygen produces
magnesium oxide.
b Potassium + water produces potassium
hydroxide and hydrogen.
c Sodium + chlorine produces sodium
chloride.

3 a $CH_4 + 2O_2 \rightarrow CO_2 + 2H_2O$
b $CH_4(g) + 2O_2(g) \rightarrow CO_2(g) + 2H_2O(l)$

Energy

PAGE 89

1 Conduction, radiation, insulation,
convection.

2 This colour does not absorb much radiation
(heat), it reflects it – the people in the car
stay cooler.

3 It traps air, which is a good insulator.

PAGE 91

1 The spider diagram should include at least
three appliances, for example, radio,
television, CD player, personal stereo.

2 Power = $\dfrac{\text{energy transferred}}{\text{time}}$

$= \dfrac{6000}{8}$

$= 750\ \text{W(atts)}$

PAGE 95

1 Non-renewable sources could include: nuclear, coal, oil and gas.
Renewable sources could include: wind, tidal, hydroelectric, solar and wood.

2 Two advantages might be that the source is renewable and doesn't produce chemical pollution.
Two disadvantages might be that they spoil the countryside and are noisy.

3 The cost of storing the radioactive waste and the cost of decomissioning a nuclear power station.

4 Flooding land to create a reservoir.

Electricity

PAGE 99

1 **a** X = resistor **b** Y = lamp **c** 4 A **d** 6 V
e 3 V

2 Cell, components.

3 **a** The current is split between the two components.
b The current is the same in the two components.

PAGE 101

1 Power $=$ potential difference (volts) $\times$ current (amps)

$= 230 \times 5$

$= 1150\ \text{W(atts)}$

2 Volts, watts, amperes.

PAGE 103

1 Rub, charge, positively, negatively.

2 Only those parts of the plate that have not been exposed to the light still have a charge and attract the black powder.

3 So that the ions are free to move the electrodes.

PAGE 105

1 The poles of the electromagnet are also reversed.

2 Two from: increase the strength of the current; increase the number of turns on the coil; place an iron core inside the coil.

PAGE 107

1 Neutral is blue, earth is green/yellow; live is brown.

2 Circuit breakers work more quickly and are reset more easily.

PAGE 109

1 Move the coil of wire faster, make the magnetic field stronger, have more turns on the coil of wire.

2 Rotated, magnetic field, lines of force, potential difference.

3 To alter the voltage.

Forces

PAGE 113

1 Speed $= \dfrac{\text{distance}}{\text{time}}$

$= \dfrac{5000}{200}$

$= 25\ \text{m/s}$

2 Acceleration $= \dfrac{\text{change in velocity}}{\text{time}}$

$= \dfrac{56 - 0}{8}$ or $\dfrac{56}{8}$

$= 7\ \text{m/s}^2$

3 Steady (constant) acceleration, then constant velocity, then constant deceleration (or negative acceleration), then stops.

PAGE 115

1 Acceleration $= \dfrac{\text{change in velocity}}{\text{time}}$

$= \dfrac{30 - 0}{5}$ or $\dfrac{30}{5}$

$= 6\ \text{m/s}^2$

2 If your mass is 60 kg you weigh about 600 N (you multiply your mass by 10).

3 **a** The forward force is greater than the backward (opposite) force.
b The backward (or opposite) force is greater than the forward force.

PAGE 117

1 Because the parachute offers much greater resistance against the force of gravity (this means it is much more difficult to pull down through the air).

2 Things which might cause a car to slow down more slowly include: the driver's reaction time, poor road conditions (for example, icy or wet) poor visibility (fog) so less time to react to situation.

3 The force of gravity and the force of friction through the air.

PAGE 119

1 It stays in orbit at a particular height above the Earth because it is travelling at a particular speed.

2 Its vision of space is not distorted by the Earth's atmosphere.

3 Geostationary – so that they always cover the same area of the Earth.

PAGE 121

1 From clouds of gas and dust collapsing under the force of gravity.

2 A star near the end of its life that has cooled and expanded by a massive amount.

3 They could tell us if life ever existed on Mars or even if it still exists.

PAGE 122

1 Work done = force × distance, therefore the work done = 200 × 450 = 90 000 J (90 kJ).

2 Potential energy stored in a spring or elastic

Waves and radiation

PAGE 125

1 a D   b A   c B.

2 Transverse: water, rope or light.
Longitudinal: springs and sound

PAGE 127

1 a

light reflected straight back

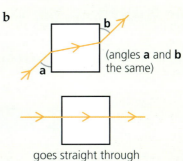
reflected at same angle (angles **a** and **b** the same)

b

(angles **a** and **b** the same)

goes straight through

2 Because the sound waves are diffracted.

PAGE 129

1 Microwaves, ultraviolet, X-rays, gamma.

2 All types of electromagnetic radiation can pass through space (a vacuum). Sound is not a type of electromagnetic radiation.

PAGE 131

1 TV controls – infra red; transmit information – radio waves; sun beds – ultraviolet; fracture pictures – X-rays.

2 They pass through soft material but not bones – they therefore make 'shadow' pictures.

3 There are many examples but one choice might be gamma rays – this type of radiation can cause cancers, on the other hand the rays can be targeted to kill cancer cells.

4 They are either 'on' or 'off'. They do not suffer interference.

PAGE 134

1 Because it will go through a great thickness of paper.

2 Gamma, alpha, beta, background.

Index